IELTS READING TESTS

(Academic Module)

McCARTER and ASH

Publishing Globally
NEW AGE INTERNATIONAL (P) LIMITED, PUBLISHERS
New Delhi • Bangalore • Chennai • Cochin • Guwahati
Hyderabad • Kolkata • Lucknow • Mumbai
Visit us at www.newagepublishers.com

First Indian Sub-Continent Edition 2006 by **New Age International (P) Ltd., Publishers**

Reprint: 2021

This special low-priced edition is for sale in **India, Bangladesh, Bhutan, Maldives, Myanmar (Bur**
Sri Lanka, Nepal and **Pakistan** only.

BRANCHES

- **Bangalore** 37/10, 8th Cross (Near Hanuman Temple), Azad Nagar, Chamarajpet, Bangalore-560 018
Tel.: (080) 26756823, Telefax: 26756820, **E-mail: bangalore@newagepublishers.com**
- **Chennai** 26, Damodaran Street, T. Nagar, Chennai-600 017
Tel.: (044) 24353401, Telefax: 24351463, **E-mail: chennai@newagepublishers.com**
- **Cochin** CC-39/1016, Carrier Station Road, Ernakulam South, Cochin-682 016
Tel.: (0484) 2377303, Telefax: 4051304, **E-mail: cochin@newagepublishers.com**
- **Guwahati** Hemsen Complex, Mohd. Shah Road, Paltan Bazar, Near Starline Hotel, Guwahati-781 008
Tel.: (0361) 2513881, Telefax: 2543669, **E-mail: guwahati@newagepublishers.com**
- **Hyderabad** 105, 1st Floor, Madhiray Kaveri Tower, 3-2-19, Azam Jahi Road, Near Kumar Theater, Nimboliadda Kachiguda, Hyderabad-500 027, Tel.: (040) 24652456, Telefax: 24652457
E-mail: hyderabad@newagepublishers.com
- **Kolkata** RDB Chambers (Formerly Lotus Cinema) 106A, 1st Floor, S.N. Banerjee Road, Kolkata-700 014
Tel.: (033) 22273773, Telefax: 22275247, **E-mail: kolkata@newagepublishers.com**
- **Lucknow** 16-A, Jopling Road, Lucknow-226 001
Tel.: (0522) 2209578, 4045297, Telefax: 2204098, **E-mail: lucknow@newagepublishers.com**
- **Mumbai** 142C, Victor House, Ground Floor, N.M. Joshi Marg, Lower Parel, Mumbai-400 013
Tel.: (022) 24927869, Telefax: 24915415, **E-mail: mumbai@newagepublishers.com**
- **New Delhi** 22, Golden House, Daryaganj, New Delhi-110 002
Tel.: (011) 23262368, 23262370, Telefax: 43551305, **E-mail: sales@newagepublishers.com**

ISBN: 978-81-224-1744-9

C-20-12-12585

Printed in India at ESS Enterprises, Rai, Haryana.

PUBLISHING GLOBALLY
NEW AGE INTERNATIONAL (P) LIMITED, PUBLISHERS
7/30 A, Daryaganj, New Delhi-110002
Visit us at **www.newagepublishers.com**
(CIN: U74899DL1966PTC004618)

Contents

Page

Acknowledgements

The authors would like to thank the following colleagues and friends for their help and support during the writing and production of this publication:

Hilary Finch, Inna Shah and Roger Townsend.

We would like to thank The British Library for permission to reproduce the extracts which appear in Reading Passage 1 in Test 7 and Reading Passage 1 in Test 8.

All of the other articles in this publication were specially commissioned for this publication and we would like to thank the following writers for their contributions:

Beatrice Barne, Beata Bart, Anthony Brown, Dr Susan Beckerleg, Lis Birrane, Margo Blythman, Samantha Carter, Dr Charles Chandler, Sandra Chandra, Barry Deedes, Beryl Dunne, Doug Foot, John Goldfinch, Peter Hopes, Dr Stepan Kuznetzov, Ruth Midgley, Sarah Moore, James Nunn, Polly Rye, Professor Mike Riley, Wendy Riley, Micky Silver, Dr Maureen Sorrel, Myrna Spatt, Dr Dave Tench, Areema Weake and Doug Young.

We would also like to thank the Cambridge Local Examinations Syndicate for permission to reproduce the Reading Answer Sheet in the Appendix.

We would also like to say a very special thank you to Drs Gill and Bruce Haddock for another sterling piece of work.

About the Authors

Sam McCarter is a lecturer in academic and medical English at Southwark College, where he organises IELTS courses for overseas doctors and other health personnel, and courses in medical English, including preparation for the OSCE component of the PLAB.

Sam McCarter is also the creator and organiser of the Nuffield Self-access Language Project for Overseas Doctors and is a free-lance consultant in medical English, specialising in tropical medicine.

Sam McCarter is co-author of **A book for IELTS,** the author of **a book on writing**, **BPP English for PLAB** and **Nuffield Stress Tests for PLAB**. He has also co-authored several other publications and edited a range of health publications.

Judith Ash is a former lecturer in academic and medical English at Southwark College. She now writes freelance and is working on distance learning programmes for IELTS and a series of IELTS books.

Judith Ash is co-author of **A book for IELTS**.

Future Publications by IntelliGene:

IntelliGene will be publishing a series of practice books for IELTS by Sam McCarter and Judith Ash. The next two books in the series will be on writing and listening.

IntelliGene will be publishing a major book on communication skills in medicine by Sam McCarter and a new book on writing skills.

Preface

This book is for students preparing for the Reading Test in the Academic Module of the International English Language Testing System (IELTS), which is administered by the British Council, the University of Cambridge Local Examinations Syndicate (UCLES) and IELTS Australia.

The book contains ten practice Reading Tests and a Key. Each Test contains three reading passages, which cover a variety of topics and give lots of practice for the range of question types used in the IELTS exam.

All the articles in this publication except for two were specially commissioned.

The book may be used as a supplement to *A Book for IELTS* by McCarter, Easton & Ash, as a supplement to a course book or for self-study.

So that you may repeat the exercises in this book, we would advise you to avoid marking the text.

Sam McCarter and Judith Ash
October 2000

The IELTS Academic Reading Module

The Reading Test in the IELTS exam lasts for 60 minutes.

The test contains three reading passages, which may include pictures, graphs, tables or diagrams. The reading passages are of different length, ranging from approximately 500 to 1,000 words. The total for the three passages is between 1,500 and 2,500 words. Each reading passage has several different types of questions, which may be printed either before or after the passage. Often the texts and the questions become more difficult as you read from Passage 1 to 3.

Reading Instructions

You should always read the instructions for each section in the reading test. The word limit, for example, in a sentence completion exercise may vary from exercise to exercise. In a heading matching exercise, you may be able to use headings more than once. So be careful!

Timing

Candidates often achieve a lower score than expected in this component of the IELTS exam, because they spend too much time on some sections and do not finish the test. It is very important to attempt to finish the test. You will not have time to read and enjoy the passages; instead, you should learn to work out what the question you are doing requires and find each answer as quickly as possible.

For many students timing is a problem. They find it difficult to leave a question that they cannot answer. This is understandable, but in the IELTS it is disastrous. While you are not answering a difficult question you could be answering two or three, or even more, easier ones. Then you can come back to those you have left blank afterwards.

Topics

The reading passage topics vary, but are all of an academic nature. Candidates sometimes panic when they are faced with a reading passage on a subject about which they know nothing at all. It is important to remember that the answers to all of the questions are in the text itself. You do not need any knowledge of the topic to be able to answer the questions. The test is designed to test your reading comprehension skills, not your knowledge of any particular subject.

Answer sheets

You must complete the answer sheet within 60 minutes. You will not have extra time to transfer your answers from the question paper to your answer sheet. Candidates often think that, because they have time to transfer their answers in the listening section, the same thing happens in the reading section. It does not.

Question type

You may have to answer any of the following question types:

Matching the two parts of split sentences

In this type of exercise, you are asked to match the two parts of split sentences. The main point here is that the completed sentence summarises the information in the reading passage. The sentence will most likely be a paraphrase of the text, so you will have to look for synonyms of the statement in the exercise.

Make sure the grammar of the two parts fits.

The completion of sentences, summaries, diagrams, tables, flow charts, notes

In this type of exercise, you are asked to complete sentences or text by using a limited number of words taken from the passage. Finding the answers is simply a matter of scanning a text for specific information. This type of question is normally used to see if you can recognise particular points of information. Note the text in the exercise, as in the other question types, may be a paraphrase of the language in the reading passage. So you should not always be looking in the passage for the same words in the stem of the sentence, but the idea expressed in another way.

You should always check what the word limit is: it may be one, two, three or four words. Remember also to make sure the words you choose fit the grammar of the sentences.

Short answers to open questions

This type of exercise is very similar to the previous one. This is simply a matter of scanning the text for specific detail. Again always check the word limit.

Multiple Choice Questions

In Multiple Choice Questions or MCQs, you are asked to choose the correct answer from four alternatives **ABCD.** Among the four alternatives **ABCD**, you will obviously have an alternative which is the correct answer. The other three alternatives can contradict the information in the passage either by stating the opposite or by giving information which although not the opposite, still contradicts the original text. For example, the reading passage may state that there are ten houses in a village and an MCQ alternative may say twenty. The information is obviously not the opposite of what is in the text. It contradicts the original text, because the information about the number is given, but it is not the same. It is interesting that students can usually see this clearly in MCQ type questions, but not when it comes to Yes/No/Not Given statements. See below.

The alternatives can also give information which does not appear in the text or information that appears in the text, but in a different context.

Note that if two alternatives have the same meaning, but are expressed in different ways, neither will be the correct answer.

Different ways to approach MCQs

❑ exclude the alternatives which you think are wrong so that you end up with only one possibility.

❑ read the stem before you read the alternatives and decide on the answer, i.e. if the stem gives you enough information. Then read the alternatives and see if you can find one to match your own answer.

❑ cover the alternatives with a piece of paper, so that you can see only the stem. Then, you can reveal the alternatives one by one. In this way, you will become less confused. Part of the problem with MCQs is the fact that you see all the information at once and it is difficult to isolate your thoughts, especially under pressure.

Yes/No/Not Given statements

In Yes/No/Not Given exercises, you have to analyse the passage by stating whether the information given in a series of statements is correct, contradictory, or if there is no information about the statement in the passage.

Students find this type of question difficult. Here are some specific hints to help you:

- Read the whole statement carefully before you make a decision.
- Look at the information in the whole statement, not part of it. For example, in the following, the information given in the exercise statement is **Yes** as regards the text.

Text: There was a rapid increase in motorbike sales over the period.
Exercise: Motorbike sales rose over the period.

Note that the text gives more information than is being asked about in the exercise. The exercise is just checking about whether the motorbike sales increased.

- Make sure you use the question **to analyse the text and not vice versa**. Look at the following:

Text: Motorbike sales rose over the period.
Exercise: There was a rapid increase in motorbike sales.

You can now see that the answer is **Not Given**. We do not know what the rate of increase was!

- Make sure you understand the three types of contradiction. Look at the following:

Text: There was a rapid increase in motorbike sales over the period.
Exercise: Motorbike sales did not rise rapidly over the period.

The answer here is obviously **No**. The contradiction in the negative is clear.

Now look at the following:

Text: There was a rapid increase in motorbike sales over the period.
Exercise: Motorbike sales rose slowly over the period.

In this case you can see that the answer is **No**. The word *slowly* contradicts the word *rapid.*

There is, however, another type of contradiction, which students quite often confuse with **Not Given.**

Text: Two types of earthworms were used to create a soil structure
Exercise: There were three types of worm used in creating a soil structure.

The answer is obviously **No.** The information about the number of worms is given clearly in the text, but the number in the exercise is different. Even though they are not opposites, they still contradict each other!

Gap-filling exercises

There are basically two types of gap-filling exercise:

- a summary of the text or part of the text with a number of blank spaces, which you complete with a word or phrase from a word list.
- a summary with a number of blank spaces without a word list, which you complete with words or phrases from the reading passage.

There are different techniques for doing this type of exercise and you may have some of your own which suit you very well. One simple aid is to read the summary through quickly to get the overall idea of the text. Then think of what kind of word you need for each blank space: an adjective, a noun, a verb, etc.

Think of your own words that will complete the meaning of the text if you can, so that when you look at the reading passage or word list, you will be able to recognise a synonym quicker.

Matching paragraph headings

In this type of exercise you are asked to match a heading to a paragraph. Many students find this type of question difficult. The following techniques may help you:

- ❑ Avoid reading the first and last sentence of a paragraph to give you the heading. This does not work in many cases. It depends on the paragraph type. For further information, see Exercises 1 – 12 in *A book for IELTS by McCarter, Easton & Ash*.
- ❑ Read each paragraph very quickly, then look away from it briefly. Decide what the main idea of the text is. If you try to read and decide at the same time, it only confuses you.
- ❑ Ask yourself why the writer wrote the paragraph. This may help you to exclude a heading which relates to minor information, and which is intended to distract you.
- ❑ Ask yourself if you can put all the information in the paragraph under the heading you have chosen.
- ❑ Check whether the heading is made up of words which are just lifted from the text. This may just be a distractor.
- ❑ Learn to distinguish between the *focus* of the paragraph and *the subsidiary or background information*, which is used to support the focus. Look at the following paragraph for example:

It is a myth that creative people are born with their talents: gifts from God or nature. Creative genius is, in fact, latent within many of us, without our realising. But how far do we need to travel to find the path to creativity? For many people, a long way. *In our everyday lives, we have to perform many acts out of habit to survive, like opening the door, shaving, getting dressed, walking to work, and so on. If this were not the case, we would, in all probability, become mentally unhinged. So strongly ingrained are our habits, though this varies from person to person, that, sometimes, when a conscious effort is made to be creative, automatic response takes over. We may try, for example, to walk to work following a different route, but end up on our usual path. By then it is too late to go back and change our minds. Another day, perhaps.* The same applies to all other areas of our lives. When we are solving problems, for example, we may seek different answers, but, often as not, find ourselves walking along the same well-trodden paths.

The text in italics above is *background or subsidiary information*. If you ask yourself why the writer wrote the paragraph, you would not answer that he wrote it to talk about our daily habits or the habits we need to survive. He is using the example *of daily habits to illustrate how they limit our creativity*. So you can see that any heading for the paragraph needs to combine two elements, namely: the limiting of creativity and the elements which set the limits. Of the two pieces of information the former is the more important of the two! Note that you should not be persuaded by the amount of text devoted to the habits.

Try this approach with any paragraph you read. In the beginning, it will slow you down. However, gradually you will learn the relationship between the various pieces of information.

- ❑ Learn to recognise different types of paragraphs. When people are reading a text for the first time they think that they know nothing about it. However, you should approach a reading passage by saying to yourself that you are aware of the overall structure of the article and you are probably aware of the organisation type of many, if not all, of the paragraphs. Look at the following paragraph:

  Although the name dinosaur is derived from the Greek for "terrible lizard", dinosaurs were not, in fact, lizards at all. Like lizards, dinosaurs are included in the class Reptilia, or reptiles, **one of the five main classes** of Vertebrata, animals with backbones. However, **at the next level of classification**, within reptiles, **significant differences** in the skeletal anatomy of lizards and dinosaurs have led scientists to place these groups of animals into **two different superorders:** Lepidosauria, or lepidosaurs, and Archosauria, or archosaurs.

Can you work out what type of paragraph this is? If this is the opening paragraph of a reading passage, what type of article do you think it is going to be? Look at the words in bold; they should help you.

Here is another example:

Reflexology is a treatment which was introduced to the West about 100 years ago, although it was practised in ancient Egypt, India and east Asia. **It involves** gently focused pressure on the feet to both diagnose and treat illness. **A reflexologist** may detect imbalances in the body on an energetic level through detecting tiny crystals on the feet. Treating these points can result in the release of blockages in other parts of the body. **It has been found to be** an especially useful treatment for sinus and upper respiratory tract conditions and poor lymphatic and cardiovascular circulation. **Anecdotal evidence from** various practitioners suggests it can also be effective in treating migraine, hormonal imbalances, digestive, circulatory and back problems.

How many times have you read paragraphs similar to this one? You may not have read any paragraphs which have exactly the same overall structure, but you will have read similar types.

It is not the purpose of this publication to set out all the different types of paragraphs. You can, however, learn to recognise different paragraph types yourself.

- ❑ Learn as much as you can about how the information in a paragraph is held together. When you are being taught how to write an essay, this is what you are being taught to do. For more information see ***a book on writing*** *by Sam McCarter* and the reading exercises in ***A book for IELTS*** *by McCarter, Easton & Ash.*

Matching information to paragraphs

This type of exercise is a variation of the previous exercise type. The exercise asks you to decide why the writer wrote the paragraphs. This, in effect, is part of the process of working out the heading for a paragraph! See above under **Matching paragraph headings**.

Test 1

Reading Passage 1

You should spend about 20 minutes on **Questions 1–15**, which are based on **Reading Passage 1** below.

Questions 1–5

Reading **Passage 1** below has 5 paragraphs **(A–E)**. Which paragraph focuses on the information below? Write the appropriate letters **(A–E)** in Boxes 1–5 on your answer sheet.

NB. Write only **ONE** letter for each answer.

1. The way parameters in the mind help people to be creative
2. The need to learn rules in order to break them
3. How habits restrict us and limit creativity
4. How to train the mind to be creative
5. How the mind is trapped by the desire for order

The creation myth

A. It is a myth that creative people are born with their talents: gifts from God or nature. Creative genius is, in fact, latent within many of us, without our realising. But how far do we need to travel to find the path to creativity? For many people, a long way. In our everyday lives, we have to perform many acts out of habit to survive, like opening the door, shaving, getting dressed, walking to work, and so on. If this were not the case, we would, in all probability, become mentally unhinged. So strongly ingrained are our habits, though this varies from person to person, that, sometimes, when a conscious effort is made to be creative, automatic response takes over. We may try, for example, to walk to work following a different route, but end up on our usual path. By then it is too late to go back and change our minds. Another day, perhaps. The same applies to all other areas of our lives. When we are solving problems, for example, we may seek different answers, but, often as not, find ourselves walking along the same well-trodden paths.

B. So, for many people, their actions and behaviour are set in immovable blocks, their minds clogged with the cholesterol of habitual actions, preventing them from operating freely, and thereby stifling creation. Unfortunately, mankind's very struggle for survival has become a tyranny – the obsessive desire to give order to the world is a case in point. Witness people's attitude to time, social customs and the panoply of rules and regulations by which the human mind is now circumscribed.

C. The groundwork for keeping creative ability in check begins at school. School, later university and then work teach us to regulate our lives, imposing a continuous process of restrictions, which is increasing exponentially with the advancement of technology. Is it surprising then that creative ability appears to be so rare? It is trapped in the prison that we have erected. Yet, even here in this hostile environment, the foundations for creativity are being laid; because setting off on the creative path is also partly about using rules and regulations. Such limitations are needed so that once they are learnt, they can be broken.

D. The truly creative mind is often seen as totally free and unfettered. But a better image is of a mind, which can be free when it wants, and one that recognises that rules and regulations are parameters, or barriers, to be raised and dropped again at will. An example of how the human mind can be trained to be creative might help here. People's minds are just like tense muscles that need to be freed up and the potential unlocked. One strategy is to erect artificial barriers or hurdles in solving a problem. As a form of stimulation, the participants in the task can be forbidden to use particular solutions or to follow certain lines of thought to solve a problem. In this way they are obliged to explore unfamiliar territory, which may lead to some startling discoveries. Unfortunately, the difficulty in this exercise, and with creation itself, is convincing people that creation is possible, shrouded as it is in so much myth and legend. There is also an element of fear involved, however subliminal, as deviating from the safety of one's own thought patterns is very much akin to madness. But, open Pandora's box, and a whole new world unfolds before your very eyes.

E. Lifting barriers into place also plays a major part in helping the mind to control ideas rather than letting them collide at random. Parameters act as containers for ideas, and thus help the mind to fix on them. When the mind is thinking laterally, and two ideas from different areas of the brain come or are brought together, they form a new idea, just like atoms floating around and then forming a molecule. Once the idea has been formed, it needs to be contained or it will fly away, so fleeting is its passage. The mind needs to hold it in place for a time so that it can recognise it or call on it again. And then the parameters can act as channels along which the ideas can flow, developing and expanding. When the mind has brought the idea to fruition by thinking it through to its final conclusion, the parameters can be brought down and the idea allowed to float off and come in contact with other ideas.

Questions 6–10

Choose the appropriate letters **A–D** and write them in Boxes 6–10 on your answer sheet.

6. According to the writer, creative people …

A are usually born with their talents
B are born with their talents
C are not born with their talents
D are geniuses

7. According to the writer, creativity is …

A a gift from God or nature
B an automatic response
C difficult for many people to achieve
D a well-trodden path

8. According to the writer, …

A the human race's fight to live is becoming a tyranny
B the human brain is blocked with cholesterol
C the human race is now circumscribed by talents
D the human race's fight to survive stifles creative ability

9. Advancing technology …

A holds creativity in check
B improves creativity
C enhances creativity
D is a tyranny

10. According to the author, creativity …

A is common
B is increasingly common
C is becoming rarer and rarer
D is a rare commodity

Questions 11–15

Do the statements below agree with the information in **Reading Passage 1**?
In Boxes 11–15, write:

Yes if the statement agrees with the information in the passage
No if the statement contradicts the information in the passage
Not Given if there is no information about the statement in the passage

Example: In some people, habits are more strongly ingrained than in others.
Answer: Yes.

11. Rules and regulations are examples of parameters.

12. The truly creative mind is associated with the need for free speech and a totally free society.

13. One problem with creativity is that people think it is impossible.

14. The act of creation is linked to madness.

15. Parameters help the mind by holding ideas and helping them to develop.

Reading Passage 2

You should spend about 20 minutes on **Questions 16–30**, which are based on **Reading Passage 2** below.

LOCKED DOORS, OPEN ACCESS

The word, "security", has both positive and negative connotations. Most of us would say that we crave security for all its positive virtues, both physical and psychological–its evocation of the safety of home, of undying love, or of freedom from need. More negatively, the word nowadays conjures up images of that huge industry which has developed to protect individuals and property from invasion by "outsiders", ostensibly malicious and intent on theft or wilful damage.

Increasingly, because they are situated in urban areas of escalating crime, those buildings which used to allow free access to employees and other users (buildings such as offices, schools, colleges or hospitals) now do not. Entry areas which in another age were called "Reception" are now manned by security staff. Receptionists, whose task it was to receive visitors and to make them welcome before passing them on to the person they had come to see, have been replaced by those whose task it is to bar entry to the unauthorized, the unwanted or the plain unappealing.

Inside, these buildings are divided into "secure zones" which often have all the trappings of combination locks and burglar alarms. These devices bar entry to the uninitiated, hinder circulation, and create parameters of time and space for user access. Within the spaces created by these zones, individual rooms are themselves under lock and key, which is a particular problem when it means that working space becomes compartmentalized.

To combat the consequent difficulty of access to people at a physical level, we have now developed technological access. Computers sit on every desk and are linked to one another, and in many cases to an external universe of other computers, so that messages can be passed to and fro. Here too security plays a part, since we must not be allowed access to messages destined for others. And so the password was invented. Now correspondence between individuals goes from desk to desk and cannot be accessed by colleagues. Library catalogues can be searched from one's desk. Papers can be delivered to, and received from, other people at the press of a button.

And yet it seems that, just as work is isolating individuals more and more, organizations are recognizing the advantages of "team-work"; perhaps in order to encourage employees to talk to one another again. Yet, how can groups work in teams if the possibilities for communication are reduced? How can they work together if e-mail provides a convenient electronic shield behind which the blurring of public and private can be exploited by the less scrupulous? If voice-mail walls up messages behind a password? If I can't leave a message on my colleague's desk because his office is locked?

Team-work conceals the fact that another kind of security, "job security", is almost always not on offer. Just as organizations now recognize three kinds of physical resources: those they buy, those they lease long-term and those they rent short-term–so it is with their human resources. Some employees have permanent contracts, some have short-term contracts, and some are regarded simply as casual labour.

Telecommunication systems offer us the direct line, which means that individuals can be contacted without the caller having to talk to anyone else. Voice-mail and the answer-phone mean that individuals can communicate without ever actually talking to one another. If we are unfortunate enough to contact an organization with a sophisticated touch-tone dialling system, we can buy things and pay for them without ever speaking to a human being.

To combat this closing in on ourselves we have the Internet, which opens out communication channels more widely than anyone could possibly want or need. An individual's electronic presence on the internet is known as the "Home Page"–suggesting the safety and security of an electronic hearth. An elaborate system of 3-dimensional graphics distinguishes this very 2-dimensional medium of "web sites". The nomenclature itself creates the illusion of a geographical entity, that the person sitting before the computer is travelling, when in fact the "site" is coming to him. "Addresses" of one kind or another move to the individual, rather than the individual moving between them, now that location is no longer geographical.

An example of this is the mobile phone. I am now not available either at home or at work, but wherever I take my mobile phone. Yet, even now, we cannot escape the security of wanting to "locate" the person at the other end. It is no coincidence that almost everyone we see answering or initiating a mobile phone-call in public begins by saying where he or she is.

Questions 16–19

Choose the appropriate letters **A–D** and write them in Boxes 16–19 on your answer sheet.

16 According to the author, one thing we long for is …

A the safety of the home
B security
C open access
D positive virtues

17. Access to many buildings …

A is unauthorised
B is becoming more difficult
C is a cause of crime in many urban areas
D used to be called 'Reception'

18. Buildings used to permit access to any users, …

A but now they do not
B and still do now
C especially offices and schools
D especially in urban areas

19. Secure zones …

A don't allow access to the user
B compartmentalise the user
C are often like traps
D are not accessible to everybody

Questions 20–27

Complete the text below, which is a summary of paragraphs 4–6. Choose your answers from the **Word List** below and write them in Boxes 20–27 on your answer sheet

There are more words and phrases than spaces, so you will not be able to use them all. You may use any word or phrase more than once.

Example:

The problem of __________ access to buildings ….

Answer: physical

The problem of physical access to buildings has now been ______20______ by technology. Messages are sent between _______21_____, with passwords not allowing _______22______ to read someone else's messages. But, while individuals are becoming increasingly ______23______ socially by the way they do their job, at the same time more value is being put on ______24______. However, e-mail and voice-mail have led to a ______25______ opportunities for person-to-person communication. And the fact that job-security is generally not available nowadays is hidden by the very concept of _______26_____. Human resources are now regarded in ______27_____ physical ones.

Word List

just the same way as	computer	cut-off
reducing of	computers	overcame
decrease in	combat	isolating
team-work	developed	physical
similar	other people	
no different from	solved	

Questions 28–30

Complete the sentences below. Use **NO MORE THAN THREE WORDS** from the passage for each answer.

Write your answers in Boxes 28 – 30 on your answer sheet.

28. The writer does not like ______________________.

29. An individual's Home Page indicates their ________________________ on the Internet.

30. Devices like mobile phones mean that location is ______________________.

Reading Passage 3

You should spend about 20 minutes on **Questions 31–40**, which are based on **Reading Passage 3** below.

National Cuisine and Tourism

To an extent, agriculture dictates that every country should have a set of specific foods which are native to that country. They may even be unique. However, even allowing for the power of agricultural science, advances in food distribution and changes in food economics to alter the ethnocentric properties of food, it is still possible for a country 'to be famous for' a particular food even if it is widely available elsewhere.

The degree to which cuisine is embedded in national culture

Within the sociology of food literature two themes suggest that food is linked to social culture. The first relates food and eating to social relationships, (Finkelstein, Vissor, Wood), and the second establishes food as a reflection of the distribution of power within social structures, (Mennell). However, establishing a role for food in personal relationships and social structures is not a sufficient argument to place food at the centre of national culture. To do that it is necessary to prove a degree of embeddedness. It would be appropriate at this point to consider the nature of culture.

The distinction made by Pierce between a behavioural contingency and a cultural contingency is crucial to our understanding of culture. Whilst a piece of behaviour may take place very often, involve a network of people and be reproducible by other networks who do not know each other, the meaning of the behaviour does not go beyond the activity itself. A cultural practice, however, contains and represents 'meta-contingencies' that is, behavioural practices that have a social meaning greater than the activity itself and which, by their nature reinforce the culture which houses them. Celebrating birthdays is a cultural practice not because everybody does it but because it has a religious meaning. Contrast this with the practice in Britain of celebrating 'Guy Fawkes Night'. It is essentially an excuse for a good time but if fireworks were banned, the occasion would gradually die away altogether or end up as cult to California. A smaller scale example might be more useful. In the British context, compare drinking in pubs with eating 'fish and chips'. Both are common practices, yet the former reflects something of the social fabric of the country, particularly family, gender, class and age relationships whilst the latter is just a national habit. In other words, a constant, well populated pattern of behaviour is not necessarily cultural. However, it is also clear that a cultural practice needs behavioural reinforcement. Social culture is not immortal.

Finkelstein argues that 'dining out' is simply 'action which supports a surface life'. For him it is the word 'out' that disconnects food from culture. This view of culture and food places the 'home' as the cultural centre. Continental European eating habits may contradict this notion by their general acceptance of eating out as part of family life. Following the principle that culture needs behavioural reinforcement, if everyone 'eats' out' on a regular basis, irrespective of social and economic differentiation, then this might constitute behavioural support for cuisine being part of social culture. That aside, the significance of a behavioural practice being embedded in culture is that it naturally maintains an approved and accepted way of life and therefore has a tendency to resist change.

The thrust of the argument is that countries differ in the degree to which their food and eating habits have a social and cultural meaning beyond the behaviour itself. This argument, however, could be interpreted to imply that the country with the greatest proportion of meals taken outside the home would be the one in which the national cuisine is more embedded in social culture. This is a difficult position to maintain because it would bring America, with its fast-food culture to the fore. The fast-food culture of America raises the issue of whether there are qualitative criteria for the concept of cuisine. The key issue is not the extent of the common behaviour but whether or not it has a function in maintaining social cohesion and is appreciated and valued through social norms. French cuisine and 'going down the pub' are strange bedfellows but bedfellows nevertheless.

How homogenous is national cuisine?

Like language, cuisine is not a static entity and whilst its fundamental character is unlikely to change in the short run it may evolve in different directions. Just as in a language there are dialects so in a cuisine there are variations. The two principal sources of diversity are the physical geography of the country and its social diversity.

The geographical dimensions work through agriculture to particularise and to limit locally produced ingredients. Ethnic diversity in the population works through the role of cuisine in social identity to create ethnically distinct cuisines which may not converge into a national cuisine. This raises the question of how far a national cuisine is related to national borders. To an ethnic group their cuisine is national. The greater the division of a society into classes, castes and status groups with their attendant ethnocentric properties, of which cuisine is a part, then the greater will be the diversity of the cuisines.

However, there is a case for convergence. Both these principal sources of diversity are, to an extent, influenced by the strength of their boundaries and the willingness of society to erode them. It is a question of isolation and integration. Efficient transport and the application of chemistry can alter agricultural boundaries to make a wider range of foods available to a cuisine. Similarly, political and social integration can erode ethnic boundaries However, all these arguments mean nothing if the cuisine is not embedded in social culture. Riley argues that when a cuisine is not embedded in social culture it is susceptible to novelty and invasion by other cuisines.

Questions 31–36

Choose one phrase **(A–K)** from the **List of phrases** to complete each **Key point** below. Write the appropriate letters **(A–K)** in Boxes 31–36 on your answer sheet.

The information in the completed sentences should be an accurate summary of the points made by the writer.

NB. There are more phrases **(A–K)** than sentences, so you will not need to use them all. You may use each phrase once only.

Key points

31. The native foods of a country, …

32. The ethnocentric properties of food …

33. Celebrating birthdays …

34. Cultural practice …

35. Drinking in pubs in Britain …

36. The link between language and cuisine …

List of phrases

A. is a behavioural practice, not a cultural practice
B. are unique
C. varies
D. is that both are diverse
E. is a reflection of the social fabric
F. is a cultural practice
G. can be changed by economic and distribution factors
H. is fundamental
I. are not as common as behaviour
J. needs to be reinforced by behaviour
K. are, to a certain extent, dictated by agriculture

Questions 37–40

Use the information in the text to match the **Authors (A–D)** with the **Findings (37–40)** below. Write the appropriate letters **(A–D)** in Boxes 37 – 40 on your answer sheet.

Authors

A **Finkelstein**

B **Pierce**

C **Mennell**

D **Riley**

Findings

37. There is a difference between behaviour and cultural practice.

38. The connection between social culture and food must be strong if national cuisine is to survive intact.

39. Distribution of power in society is reflected in food.

40. The link between culture and eating outside the home is not strong.

Test 2

Reading Passage 1

You should spend about 20 minutes on **Questions 1–14**, which are based on **Reading Passage 1** below.

TEA TIMES

A. The chances are that you have already drunk a cup or glass of tea today. Perhaps, you are sipping one as you read this. Tea, now an everyday beverage in many parts of the world, has over the centuries been an important part of rituals of hospitality both in the home and in wider society.

B. Tea originated in China, and in Eastern Asia tea making and drinking ceremonies have been popular for centuries. Tea was first shipped to North Western Europe by English and Dutch maritime traders in the sixteenth century. At about the same time, a land route from the Far East, via Moscow, to Europe was opened up. Tea also figured in America's bid for independence from British rule–the Boston Tea Party.

C. As, over the last four hundred years, tea-leaves became available throughout much of Asia and Europe, the ways in which tea was drunk changed. The Chinese considered the quality of the leaves and the ways in which they were cured all important. People in other cultures added new ingredients besides tea-leaves and hot water. They drank tea with milk, sugar, spices like cinnamon and cardamom, and herbs such as mint or sage. The variations are endless. For example, in Western Sudan on the edge of the Sahara Desert, sesame oil is added to milky tea on cold mornings. In England tea, unlike coffee, acquired a reputation as a therapeutic drink that promoted health. Indeed, in European and Arab countries as well as in Persia and Russia, tea was praised for its restorative and health giving properties. One Dutch physician, Cornelius Blankaart, advised that to maintain health a minimum of eight to ten cups a day should be drunk, and that up to 50 to 100 daily cups could be consumed with safety.

D. While European coffee houses were frequented by men discussing politics and closing business deals, respectable middle-class women stayed at home and held tea parties. When the price of tea fell in the nineteenth century poor people took up the drink with enthusiasm. Different grades and blends of tea were sold to suit every pocket.

E. Throughout the world today, few religious groups object to tea drinking. In Islamic cultures, where drinking of alcohol is forbidden, tea and coffee consumption is an important part of social life. However, Seventh-Day Adventists, recognising the beverage as a drug containing the stimulant caffeine, frown upon the drinking of tea.

F. Nomadic Bedouin are well known for traditions of hospitality in the desert. According to Middle Eastern tradition, guests are served both tea and coffee from pots kept ready on the fires of guest tents where men of the family and male visitors gather. Cups of 'bitter' cardamom coffee and glasses of sugared tea should be constantly refilled by the host.

G. For over a thousand years, Arab traders have been bringing Islamic culture, including tea drinking, to northern and western Africa. Techniques of tea preparation and the ceremonial involved have been adapted. In West African countries, such as Senegal and The Gambia, it is fashionable for young men to gather in small groups to brew Chinese 'gunpowder' tea. The tea is boiled with large amounts of sugar for a long time.

H. Tea drinking in India remains an important part of daily life. There, tea made entirely with milk is popular. 'Chai' is made by boiling milk and adding tea, sugar and some spices. This form of tea making has crossed the Indian Ocean and is also popular in East Africa, where tea is considered best when it is either very milky or made with water only. Curiously, this 'milk or water' formula has been carried over to the preparation of instant coffee, which is served in cafes as either black, or sprinkled on a cup of hot milk.

I. In Britain, coffee drinking, particularly in the informal atmosphere of coffee shops, is currently in vogue. Yet, the convention of afternoon tea lingers. At conferences, it remains common practice to serve coffee in the morning and tea in the afternoon. Contemporary China, too, remains true to its long tradition. Delegates at conferences and seminars are served tea in cups with lids to keep the infusion hot. The cups are topped up throughout the proceedings. There are as yet no signs of coffee at such occasions.

Questions 1–8

Reading Passage 1 has 9 paragraphs **(A–I)**. Choose the most suitable heading for each paragraph from the **List of headings** below. Write the appropriate numbers **(i–xiii)** in Boxes 1–8 on your answer sheet.

One of the headings has been done for you as an example.

NB. There are more headings than paragraphs, so you will not use all of them.

1. **Paragraph A**
2. **Paragraph B**
3. **Paragraph C**
4. **Paragraph D**
5. **Paragraph E**

Example **Paragraph F** Answer: xiii

6. **Paragraph G**
7. **Paragraph H**
8. **Paragraph I**

List of headings

i. Diverse drinking methods
ii Limited objections to drinking tea
iii Today's continuing tradition – in Britain and China
iv Tea – a beverage of hospitality
v An important addition – tea with milk
vi Tea and alcohol
vii The everyday beverage in all parts of the world
viii Tea on the move
ix African tea
x The fall in the cost of tea
xi The value of tea
xii Tea-drinking in Africa
xiii Hospitality among the Bedouin

Questions 9–14

Complete the sentences below. Use **NO MORE THAN THREE WORDS** from the passage to complete each blank space.

9. For centuries, both at home and in society, tea has had an important role in ________.

10. Falling tea prices in the nineteenth century meant that people could choose the ________________ of tea they could afford.

11. Because it ________________ Seventh-Day Adventists do not approve of the drinking of tea.

12. In the desert, one group that is well known for its traditions of hospitality is the ________________.

13. In India, ________________, as well as tea, are added to boiling milk to make 'chai'.

14. In Britain, while coffee is in fashion, afternoon tea is still a ______________.

Reading Passage 2

You should spend about 20 minutes on **Questions 15–29**, which are based on **Reading Passage 2** below.

Tyes and Greens

There are a number of settlements in this part of East Anglia with names containing the word 'tye'. The word is Anglo-Saxon in origin, and the Oxford English Dictionary quotes the earliest usage of the term as dating from 832. Essentially a 'tye' was a green, or a small area of open common land, usually sited away from the main village or settlement, perhaps at the junction of two or more routes. Local people and passing travellers had the right to pasture their horses, pigs and other farm animals on the tye.

In the Pebmarsh area there seem to have been five or six of these tyes, all, except one, at the margins of the parish. These marginal clearings are all away from the richer farming land close to the river, and, in the case of Cooks Green, Hayles Tye, and Dorking Tye, close to the edge of still existing fragments of ancient woodland. It seems likely then that, here, as elsewhere in East Anglia, medieval freemen were allowed to clear a small part of the forest and create a smallholding. Such unproductive forest land would, in any case, have been unattractive to the wealthy baronial or monastic landowners. Most of the land around Pebmarsh village belonged to Earls Colne Priory, a wealthy monastery about 10 kilometres to the south, and it may be that by the 13th and 14th centuries the tyes were maintained by tenant farmers paying rent to the Priory.

Hayles Tye seems to have got its name from a certain John Hayle who is documented in the 1380s, although there are records pointing to occupation of the site at a much earlier date. The name was still in use in 1500, and crops up again throughout the 16th and 17th centuries, usually in relation to the payment of taxes or tithes. At some point during the 18th century the name is changed to File's Green, though no trace of an owner called File has been found. Also in the 18th century the original dwellings on the site disappeared. Much of this region was economically depressed during this period and the land and its dwellings may simply have been abandoned. Several farms were abandoned in the neighbouring village of Alphamstone, and the population dwindled so much that there was no money to support the fabric of the village church, which became very dilapidated. However, another possibility is that the buildings at File's Green burnt down, fires being not infrequent at this time.

By 1817 the land was in the ownership of Charles Townsend of Ferriers Farm, and in 1821 he built two brick cottages on the site, each cottage occupied by two families of agricultural labourers. The structure of these cottages was very simple, just a two-storey rectangle divided in the centre by a large common chimney piece. Each dwelling had its own fireplace, but the two families seem to have shared a brick bread-oven which jutted out from the rear of the cottage. The outer wall of the bread-oven is still visible on the remaining cottage. The fireplaces themselves and the chimney structure appear to be older than the 1821 cottages and may have survived from the earlier dwellings. All traces of the common land had long disappeared, and the two cottages stood on a small plot of less than an acre where the labourers would have been able to grow a few vegetables and keep a few chickens or a pig. The bulk of their time was spent working at Ferriers farm.

Both cottages are clearly marked on maps of 1874, but by the end of the century one of them had gone. Again, the last years of the 19th century were a period of agricultural depression, and a number of smaller farms in the area were abandoned. Traces of one, Mosse's Farm, still partly encircled by a very overgrown moat, may be seen less than a kilometre from File's Green. It seems likely that, as the need for agricultural labour declined, one of the cottages fell into disuse, decayed and was eventually pulled down. Occasional fragments of rubble and brick still surface in the garden of the remaining cottage.

In 1933, this cottage was sold to the manager of the newly-opened gravel works to the north-west of Pebmarsh village. He converted these two dwellings into one. This, then, is the only remaining habitation on the site, and is called File's Green Cottage.

Questions 15–18

Choose the appropriate letters **A–D** and write them in Boxes 15–18 on your answer sheet.

15. A tye was ...

A a green
B a large open area
C common land with trees
D found at the junction of two or more routes

16. The Pebmarsh area ...

A probably had seven tyes
B probably had six tyes
C appears to have had five or six tyes
D was not in East Anglia

17. The tyes in the Pebmarsh area were ...

A near the river
B used by medieval freemen
C mostly at the margins of the parish
D owned by Earls Colne Priory

8. According to the writer, wealthy landowners ...

A did not find the sight of forest land attractive
B found the sight of forest land attractive
C were attracted by the sight of forest land
D considered forest land unproductive

Questions 19–29

Complete the text below, which is a summary of paragraphs 3 – 6 in Reading Passage 2. Use **NO MORE THAN THREE WORDS** from the passage to fill each blank space.

Write your answers in Boxes 19 – 29 on your answer sheet.

1380s– John Hayle, who is __________19__________, apparently gave his name to Hayles Tye.

1500s– the name of Hayles Tye was still __________20__________, __________21__________ again in the following two centuries in relation to taxes.

18th century- Hayles Tye was renamed __________22__________; the original dwellings may either have disappeared, or were __________23__________.

1817 - the land was __________24__________ by Charles Townsend.

1821– Charles Townsend built __________25__________ cottages on the site, __________26__________ inhabited by two families, but by the end of the nineteenth century only one cottage __________27__________.

1933 – The cottage, now called File's Green Cottage, was bought by the local __________28__________ manager who converted the cottage into __________29__________.

Reading Passage 3

You should spend about 20 minutes on **Questions 30–40**, which are based on **Reading Passage 3** below.

Haydn's late quartets

By the time he came to write the String Quartets published as Opus 76 and Opus 77, Haydn was undoubtedly the most famous living composer in the whole of Europe. He had recently returned from the highly successful second visit to England, for which he had composed his last six symphonies, culminating in the brilliant and festive Drum Roll Symphony (No. 103) and London Symphony (No. 104). This is public music, full of high spirits, expansive gestures and orchestral surprises. Haydn knew how to please his audience. And in 1796, following his return to Vienna, he began work on his largest and most famous choral work, the oratorio, 'The Creation'. In the succeeding years, till 1802, he was to write a series of other large scale religious choral works, including several masses. The oratorios and masses were also public works, employing large forces for dramatic effect, but warm and full of apparently spontaneous religious feeling. Yet at the same time he composed these 8 quartets, in terms of technical mastery and sheer musical invention the equal of the symphonies and choral works, but in their mood and emotional impact far removed, by turns introspective and detached, or full of passionate intensity.

Once again, as in the early 1770s when he appears to have been going through some kind of spiritual crisis, Haydn returned to the String Quartet as a means to accomplish a twofold aim: firstly to innovate musically in a genre free from public performance requirements or religious convention; secondly to express personal emotions or philosophy in a musical form that is intimate yet capable of great subtlety and complexity of meaning. The result is a series of quartets of astonishing structural, melodic, rhythmic and harmonic variety, inhabiting a shifting emotional world, where tension underlies surface brilliance and calm gives way to unease.

The six quartets of Opus 76 differ widely in character. The opening movement of No. 2 is tense and dramatic while that of No 4 begins with the soaring long-breathed melody that has earned it the nickname of 'The Sunrise'. The minuets too have moved a long way from the stately court dance of the mid-eighteenth century. The so-called 'Witches Minuet' of No. 2 is a strident canon, that of No. 6 is a fast one-in-a-bar movement anticipating the scherzos of Beethoven, while at the heart of No. 5 is a contrasting trio section which, far from being the customary relaxed variant of the surrounding minuet, flings itself into frenetic action and is gone. The finales are full of the energy and grace we associate with Haydn, but with far less conscious humour and more detachment than in earlier quartets.

But it is in the slow movements that Haydn is most innovative and most unsettling. In No. 1 the cello and the first violin embark on a series of brusque dialogues. No.4 is a subdued meditation based on the hushed opening chords. The slow movements of No.5 and No.6 are much looser in structure, the cello and viola setting off on solitary episodes of melodic and harmonic uncertainty. But there the similarity ends, for while No.5 is enigmatic, and predominantly dark in tone, the overlapping textures of its sister are full of light-filled intensity.

The Opus 76 quartets were published in 1799, when Haydn was well over 60 years old. Almost immediately he was commissioned to write another set by Prince Lobkowitz, a wealthy patron, who was later to become an important figure in Beethoven's life. Two quartets only were completed and published as Opus 77 Nos 1 & 2 in 1802. But these are not the works of an old man whose powers are fading, or who simply consolidates ground already covered. Once again Haydn innovates. The opening movement of Opus 77 No.2 is as structurally complex and emotionally unsettling as anything he ever wrote, alternating between a laconic opening theme and a tense and threatening counter theme which comes to dominate the whole movement. Both quartets have fast scherzo-like 'minuets'. The slow movement of No.1 is in traditional variation form, but stretches the form to the limit in order to accommodate widely contrasting textures and moods. The finale of No.2 is swept along by a seemingly inexhaustible stream of energy and inventiveness.

In fact, Haydn began a third quartet in this set, but never finished it, and the two completed movements were published in 1806 as Opus 103, his last published work. He was over 70, and clearly lacked the strength to continue composition. The two existing movements are a slow movement followed by a minuet. The slow movement has a quiet warmth, but it is the minuet that is remarkable. It is in true dance time, unlike the fast quasi-scherzos of the earlier quartets. But what a dance! In a sombre D minor Haydn unfolds an angular, ruthless little dance of death. The central trio section holds out a moment of consolation, and then the dance returns, sweeping on relentlessly to the final sudden uprush of sound. And then, after more than 40 years of composition the master falls silent.

Questions 30–32

Choose the appropriate letters **A–D** and write them in Boxes 30–32 on your answer sheet.

30. Which one of the following statements is true?

A Haydn wrote the London Symphony in England
B We do not know where Haydn wrote the London Symphony
C Haydn wrote the London Symphony in Vienna
D Haydn wrote the Drum Roll Symphony in England

31. Like symphonies 103 and 104, the oratorios and masses were ...

A written in the eighteenth century
B for the public
C as emotional as the quartets
D full of religious feeling

32. The string quartets in Opus 76 and Opus 77 were ...

A the cause of a spiritual crisis
B intimate yet capable
C calm unease
D diverse

Questions 33–37

Complete the text below, which is a summary of paragraphs 3 and 4 in Reading Passage 3. Choose your answers from the **Word List** below and write them in Boxes 33–37 on your answer sheet.

There are more words and phrases than spaces, so you will not be able to use them all. You may use each word or phrase only once.

Example: The six quartets of Opus 76 are very __________.

Answer: different.

For example, the opening of 'The Sunrise' is not nearly as _____33_____ as that of No. 2. _____34_____ those of the mid-eighteenth century, the minuets are more frenetic and less relaxed. It is in the slow movements, however, that Haydn tried something very different. In contrast to No. 4, No. 1 is much _____35_____ brusque, the former being much _____36_____. _____37_____, Nos. 5 and 6 are alike in some respects.

Word List

wide	less	different
more	long-breathed	unlike
similarly	subdued	tense
like	conversely	quieter

Questions 38–40

Do the statements below agree with the information in **Reading Passage 3**?
In Boxes 38–40, write:

Yes if the statement agrees with the information in the passage
No if the statement contradicts the information in the passage
Not Given if there is no information about the statement in the passage

Example: Haydn was well-known when he wrote Opus 76.

Answer: Yes.

38. Before the Opus 76 quartets were published, Haydn had been commissioned to write more.

39. The writer says that Opus 103 was Haydn's last published work.

40. The writer admires Haydn for the diversity of the music he composed.

Test 3

Reading Passage 1

You should spend about 20 minutes on **Questions 1–14**, which are based on **Reading Passage 1** below.

The politics of pessimism

Newspaper headlines and TV or radio news bulletins would have us believe erroneously that a new age has come upon us, the Age of Cassandra. People are being assailed not just with contemporary doom, or past gloom, but with prophecies of disasters about to befall. The dawn of the new millennium has now passed; the earth is still intact, and the *fin de siècle* Jeremiahs have now gone off to configure a new date for the apocalypse.

It can, I believe, be said with some certainty that the doom-mongers will never run out of business. Human nature has an inclination for pessimism and anxiety, with each age having its demagogues, foretelling doom or dragging it in their wake. But what makes the modern age so different is that the catastrophes are more 'in your face'. Their assault on our senses is relentless. Whether it be sub-conscious or not, this is a situation not lost on politicians. They play upon people's propensity for unease, turning it into a very effective political tool.

Deluding the general public

All too often, when politicians want to change the status quo, they take advantage of people's fears of the unknown and their uncertainties about the future. For example, details about a new policy may be leaked to the press. Of course, the worst case scenario is presented in all its depressing detail. When the general public reacts in horror, the government appears to cave in. And then accepting some of the suggestions from their critics, ministers water down their proposals. This allows the government to get what it wants, while at the same time fooling the public into believing that they have *got one over on* the government. Or even that they have some say in the making of policy.

There are several principles at play here. And both are rather simple: unsettle people and then play on their fears; and second, people must be given an opportunity to make a contribution, however insignificant, in a given situation; otherwise, they become dissatisfied, not fearful or anxious.

A similar ruse, at a local level, will further illustrate how easily people's base fears are exploited. A common practice is to give people a number of options, say in a housing development, ranging from no change to radical transformation of an area. The aim is to persuade people to agree significant modifications, which may involve disruption to their lives, and possibly extra expenditure. The individuals, fearful of the worst possible outcome, plump for the middle course. And this, incidentally, is invariably the option favoured by the authorities. Every thing is achieved under the guise of market research. But it is obviously a blatant exercise in the manipulation of people's fears.

Fear and survival

Fear and anxieties about the future affect us all. People are wracked with self-doubt and low self-esteem. In the struggle to exist and advance in life, a seemingly endless string of obstacles is encountered, so many, in fact, that any accomplishment seems surprising. Even when people do succeed, they are still nagged by uncertainty.

Not surprisingly, feelings like doubt, fear, anxiety and pessimism are usually associated with failure. Yet, if properly harnessed, they are the driving force behind success, the very engines of genius.

If things turn out well for a long time, there is a further anxiety: that of constantly waiting for something to go wrong. People then find themselves propitiating the gods: not walking on lines on the pavements, performing rituals before public performances, wearing particular clothes and colours so that they can blame the ritual not themselves when things go wrong.

But surely the real terror comes when success continues uninterrupted for such a long period of time that we forget what failure is like!

We crave for and are fed a daily diet of anxiety. Horror films and disaster movies have an increasing appeal. Nostradamus pops his head up now and again. And other would-be prophets make a brief appearance, predicting the demise of human kind. Perhaps, this is all just a vestige of the hardships of early man–our attempt to recreate the struggles of a past age, as life becomes more and more comfortable.

Mankind cannot live by contentment alone. And so, a world awash with anxieties and pessimism has been created. Being optimistic is a struggle. But survival dictates that mankind remain ever sanguine.

Questions 1–5

Choose one phrase **(A–K)** from the **List of phrases** to complete each **Key point** below. Write the appropriate letters **(A–K)** in Boxes 1–5 on your answer sheet.

The information in the completed sentences should be an accurate summary of the points made by the writer.

NB. There are more phrases **(A–K)** than sentences, so you will not need to use them all. You may use each phrase once only.

Key points

1. Newspaper headlines and TV or radio news bulletins …
2. Doom-mongers are popular, because people …
3. Today, catastrophes …
4. To politicians, people's inclination for fear …
5. The government …

List of phrases

A are not as threatening as in the past
B tell the truth
C blame them
D try to make us believe mistakenly that we are in a new era
E calm people down
F are uncertain about the future
G are less comfortable
H are natural pessimists and worriers
I are more immediate
J get what they want by deceiving the public
K is something they can make use of

Questions 6–9

Choose the appropriate letters **A–D** and write them in Boxes 6–9 on your answer sheet.

6. The housing development example shows that people …

A are not that easily deceived
B like market research
C lead their fears
D are easy to delude

7. Which one of the following statements is true, according to the passage?

   A Market research uses people's fears for their own good
   B People are scared by market research techniques
   C Market research techniques are used as a means of taking advantage of people's fears
   D Market research makes people happy

8. The engines of genius are …

   A properly harnessed
   B the driving force behind success
   C driven by feelings like fear
   D usually associated with failure

9. Continual success …

   A makes people arrogant
   B worries people
   C does not have any negative effects on people
   D increases people's self-esteem

Questions 10–14

Do the statements below agree with the information in **Reading Passage 1**?
In Boxes 10–14, write:

Yes if the statement agrees with the information in the passage
No if the statement contradicts the information in the passage
Not Given if there is no information about the statement in the passage

Example: Politicians pretend things are worse than they are.

Answer: Yes.

10. The complex relationship between failure and success needs to be addressed carefully.

11. People perform certain rituals to try to avoid failure.

12. Anxiety in daily life is what we want.

13. The writer believes that Nostradamus and certain other prophets are right about their predictions for the end of the human race.

14. Mankind needs to be pessimistic to survive.

Reading Passage 2

You should spend about 20 minutes on **Questions 15–28**, which are based on **Reading Passage 2** below.

Caveat scriptor!

Let the would-be writer beware! Anyone foolhardy enough to embark on a career as a writer–whether it be an academic treatise, a novel, or even an article–should first read this!

People think that writing as a profession is glamorous; that it is just about sitting down and churning out words on a page, or more likely these days on a computer-screen. If only it were! So what exactly does writing a book entail? Being a writer is about managing a galaxy of contradictory feelings: elation, despair, hope, frustration, satisfaction and depression–and not all separately! Of course, it also involves carrying out detailed research: first to establish whether there is a market for the planned publication, and second into the content of the book. Sometimes, however, instinct takes the place of market research and the contents are dictated not by plans and exhaustive research, but by experience and knowledge.

Once the publication has been embarked upon, there is a long period of turmoil as the text takes shape. A first draft is rarely the final text of the book. Nearly all books are the result of countless hours of altering and re-ordering chunks of text and deleting the embarrassing bits. While some people might think that with new technology the checking and editing process is speeded up, the experienced writer would hardly agree. Unfortunately, advanced technology now allows the writer the luxury of countless editings; a temptation many of us find hard to resist. So a passage, endlessly re-worked may end up nothing remotely like the original, and completely out of place when compared with the rest of the text.

After the trauma of self-editing and looking for howlers, it is time to show the text to other people, friends perhaps, for appraisal. At this stage, it is not wise to send it off to a literary agent or direct to publishers, as it may need further fine-tuning of which the author is unaware. Once an agent has been approached and has rejected a draft publication, it is difficult to go and ask for the re-vamped text to be considered again. It also helps, at this stage, to offer a synopsis of the book, if it is a novel, or an outline if it is a textbook. This acts as a guide for the author, and a general reference for friends and later for agents.

Although it is tempting to send the draft to every possible agent at one time, it is probably unwise. Some agents may reject the publication out of hand, but others may proffer some invaluable advice, for example about content or the direction to be taken. Hints like this may be of use in finally being given a contract by an agent or publisher.

The lucky few taken on by publishers or agents, then have their books subjected to a number of readers, whose job it is to vet a book: deciding whether it is worth publishing and whether the text as it stands is acceptable or not. After a book has finally been accepted by a publisher, one of the greatest difficulties for the writer lies in taking on board the publisher's alterations to the text. Whilst the overall story and thrust of the book may be acceptable, it will probably have to conform to an in-house style, as regards language, spelling, or punctuation, etc. More seriously, the integrity of the text may be challenged, and this may require radical re-drafting which is unpalatable to the author. A book's creation period is complex and unnerving, but the publisher's reworkings and text amputations can also be a tortuous process.

For many writers, the most painful period comes when the text has been accepted, and the writer is waiting for it to be put together for the printer. By this stage, it is not uncommon for the writer to be thoroughly sick of the text.

Abandon writing? Nonsense. Once smitten, it is not easy to escape the compulsion to create and write, despite the roller-coaster ride of contradictory emotions.

Questions 15–22

Complete the text below, which is a summary of the passage. Choose your answers from the **Word List** below and write them in Boxes 15–22 on your answer sheet.

There are more words and phrases than spaces, so you will not be able to use them all. You may use each word or phrase only once.

Example: Anyone who wants to be a writer should __________.

Answer: beware.

People often associate writing with __________15__________. But being a writer involves managing conflicting emotions as well as __________16__________ or instinct. Advanced technology, contrary to what might be thought, does not make the __________17__________ faster.

When a writer has a draft of the text ready, it is a good idea to have a __________18__________ for friends, etc to look at. If an author is accepted by a publisher, the draft of the book is given to __________19__________ for vetting. __________20__________ are then often made, which are not easy for the writer to agree.

However, __________21__________ is compelling, even though there are __________22__________.

Word List

editing process	beware	readers
first draft	glamour	a literary agent
alterations	profession	publisher
challenges	writing	dictating
research	publishing	summary
ups and downs	roller-coaster	

Questions 23 and 24

Choose the appropriate letters **A–D** and write them in Boxes 23 and 24 on your answer sheet.

23. In the planning stages of a book, …

A instinct can replace market research
B market research can replace instinct
C market research is essential
D instinct frequently replaces market research

24. The problem with the use of advanced technology in editing is that …

   A it becomes different from the original
   B it is unfortunate
   C it is a luxury
   D many writers cannot resist changing the text again and again

Questions 25–28

Complete the sentences below. Use **NO MORE THAN THREE WORDS** from the passage to complete each blank space.

25. Once a text is finished, the writer needs to get the ____________ of other people.

26. Some agents may reject the draft of a book, while others may offer _________.

27. Apart from the need for a draft to conform to an in-house style, a publisher's changes to a text may include ____________.

28. The publisher's alterations to a book are difficult for a writer, as is the ___________ as the book grows.

Reading Passage 3

You should spend about 20 minutes on **Questions 29–40**, which are based on **Reading Passage 3** below.

Leisure time

A. A raft of forecasts has been made in recent decades, predicting the decline in the number of working hours coupled with a consequent increase in leisure time. It was estimated that the leisure revolution would take place by the turn of the last century with hours devoted to work falling to 25–30 per week. This reduction has failed to materialise, but the revolution has, nonetheless, arrived.

B. Over the past 30 to 40 years, spending on leisure has witnessed a strong increase. According to the annual family expenditure survey published in 1999 by the Office for National Statistics, the average household in the United Kingdom spent more on leisure than food, housing and transport for the very first time. And the trend is also set to continue upwards well into the present century.

C. The survey, based on a sample of 6,500 households showed, that the days are long gone when the average family struggled to buy basic foods. As recently as 1960, family spending on food was approximately one third compared to 17% now. Twelve years later, there was a noticeable shift towards leisure with the percentage of household spending on leisure increasing to 9%, and that on food declining to 26%.

D. The average household income in the UK in 1999 was £460 per week before tax, and average spending was £352.20. Of the latter sum, £59.70 was spent on leisure and £58.90 on food. On holidays alone, family expenditure was 6%, while in 1969 the proportion spent on holidays was just 2%. And whereas the richest 10% lashed out 20% of their income in 1999 on leisure, the poorest spent 12%.

E. Among the professional and managerial classes, working hours have increased and, overall in the economy, record numbers of people are in employment. As people work more, the appetite for leisure activities has grown to compensate for the greater stress in life. The past 5 years alone have seen the leisure business expand by 25% with a change in emphasis to short domestic week-end breaks, and long-haul short breaks to exotic destinations in place of long holidays. In the future, it is expected that people will jump from one leisure activity to another in complexes catering for everyone's needs with gyms, cinemas, cafes, restaurants, bars and internet facilities all under one roof. The leisure complexes of today will expand to house all the leisure facilities required for the leisure age.

F. Other factors fueling demand for leisure activities are rising prosperity, increasing longevity and a more active elderly population. Hence, at the forefront of leisure spending are not just the young or the professional classes. The 1999 family expenditure survey showed that the 64 to 75 year-old group spend a higher proportion of their income on leisure than any other age group. The strength of the 'grey pound' now means that elderly people are able to command more respect and, thus, attention in the leisure market.

G. And the future? It is anticipated that, in the years to come, leisure spending will account for between a third to a half of all household spending, Whilst it is difficult to give exact figures, the leisure industry will certainly experience a long period of sustained growth. Working hours are not expected to decrease, partly because the 24-hour society will need to be serviced; and secondly, because more people will be needed to keep the service/leisure industries running.

H. In the coming decades, the pace of change will accelerate, generating greater wealth at a faster rate than even before. Surveys show that this is already happening in many parts of Europe. The south-east of England, for example, is now supposedly the richest area in the EEC. The 'leisure pound' is one of the driving forces behind this surge. But, sadly, it does not look as if we will have the long leisure hours that we had all been promised.

Questions 29–35

Reading Passage 3 has 8 paragraphs **(A–H)**. Choose the most suitable heading for each paragraph from the **List of headings** below. Write the appropriate numbers **(i–xiv)** in Boxes 29 -35 on your answer sheet.
One of the headings has been done for you as an example.

You may use any heading more than once.

NB. There are more headings than paragraphs, so you will not use all of them.

29. **Paragraph A**
30. **Paragraph B**
31. **Paragraph C**

Example **Paragraph D**

Answer: iv

32. **Paragraph E**
33. **Paragraph F**
34. **Paragraph G**
35. **Paragraph H**

List of headings

i. Leisure spending goes up strongly
ii Decreasing unemployment
iii False forecasts
iv Spending trends–leisure v food
v More affordable food
vi Leisure as an answer to stress
vii Looking forward
viii The leisure revolution–working hours reduced to 25
ix The 'grey pound' soars
x Rising expenditure
xi The elderly leisure market
xii National Statisticians
xiii Work, stress, and leisure all on the up
xiv Money yes, leisure time no

Questions 36–40

Do the statements below agree with the information in **Reading Passage 3**?
In Boxes 36–40, write:

Yes if the statement agrees with the information in the passage
No if the statement contradicts the information in the passage
Not Given if there is no information about the statement in the passage

Example: In recent decades, an increase in working hours was predicted.

Answer: No.

36. At the turn of the last century, weekly work hours dropped to 25.

37. Spending on leisure has gone up over the past three decades.

38. Long holidays have taken the place of long-haul short breaks.

39. In future, people will pay less for the leisure facilities they use than they do today.

40. The 24-hour society will have a negative effect on people's attitudes to work.

Test 4

Reading Passage 1

You should spend about 20 minutes on **Questions 1–14**, which are based on **Reading Passage 1** below.

In or out?

British further education colleges did not traditionally have any concerns about student drop-out, because the origins of the sector were in vocational apprenticeship training for employers where the apprentices could not drop out without endangering their job. In the 70s, this sector began to expand into more general education courses, which were seen both as an alternative to school for 16–18 year-olds and a second chance for adults. The philosophy was mainly liberal with students regarded as adults who should not be heavily monitored, but rather free to make their own decisions; it was not uncommon to hear academic staff argue that attendance at classes was purely voluntary.

In the 80s, with an increased consciousness of equal opportunities, the focus of the further education colleges moved to widening participation, encouraging into colleges students from previously under-represented groups, particularly from ethnic minorities. This, in turn, led to a curriculum which was more representative of the new student body. For example, there were initiatives to ensure the incorporation of literature by black writers into A-level literature courses; history syllabuses were altered to move beyond a purely Eurocentric view of the world; and geography syllabuses began to look at the politics of maps.

A turning point came in 1991 with the publication of a report on completion rates by the government inspection body for education, Her Majesty's Inspectorate for England and Wales, (HMI 1991). However, this report was based on academic staff's explanations of why students had left. It suggested that the vast majority left either for personal reasons or because they had found employment and that only 10% left for reasons that could in any way be attributed to the college.

Meanwhile, Britain had been going through the Thatcherite revolution and, in parallel to the Reagan politics of the US, a key principle was the need to reduce taxation drastically. At this point (and to a large extent still), further and higher education colleges were almost entirely funded from the public purse. There had been many cuts in this funding through the 80s, but no one had really looked at value for money. However, in the early 90s, the Audit Commission with Office of Standards in Education (OFSTED) (the new version of HMI) turned the spotlight onto further education and published a seminal report, *Unfinished Business* (Audit Commission and OFSTED 1993), which showed that drop-out was happening on a significant scale and, crucially given the politics of the time, attributed a cost to the state of £500 million, arguing that this was a waste of public (i.e. taxpayers') money. To quote Yorke (1999), non-completion became political. The Audit Commission report coincided with government moves to privatise the functions of the state as much as possible; and with the decision to remove further education from the control of local government and give it a quasi-dependent status, where colleges were governed by independent boards of governors bidding to the state for funding to run educational provision. As part of this, a new series of principles for funding and bidding were developed (FEFC 1994) which incorporated severe financial penalties for student drop-out. In essence, the system is that almost all the state funding is attached to the individual student. There is funding for initial advice and guidance, on-course delivery and student achievement, but if the student drops out, the college loses that funding immediately, so that loss of students in the first term leads to an immediate loss of college funding for the other two terms. Not surprisingly, this focused the concern of colleges immediately and sharply on the need to improve student retention rates.

Recently, therefore, there has been considerable effort to improve retention but, as Martinez (1995) pointed out, there was no body of research on which to base strategies. An additional complexity was that colleges had been slow to computerise their student data and most colleges were in the position of not knowing what their retention rates were or any patterns involved. Where data did exist it was held separately by either administrative or academic staff with poor communication between these groups. Colleges, however, jumped into a number of strategies based largely on experience, instinct and common sense and publication of these began. (Martinez 1996; Martinez 1997; Kenwright 1996; Kenwright 1997)

The main strategies tried are outlined in the literature as summarised by Martinez (1996). These include sorting activities around entry to ensure 'best fit', supporting activities including child care, financial support and enrichment/learner support, connecting activities to strengthen the relationship between the college and the student, including mentoring and tutorials and activities to transform the student, including raising of expectations and study/career development support and tutoring.

Questions 1–3

Use the information in the text to match the each of the **years** listed **(1–3)** with one of the **Key events in the development of further education (i–vii)**. Write the appropriate letter in **Boxes 1–3** on your answer sheet. Note that there are more items listed under the **Key events** than **years**, so you will not use all of them.

Years

1. 1991
2. 1993
3. 1994

Key events in the development of further education

i. Severe penalties for drop-out are developed as part of college funding mechanisms
ii. Serious attempts are made to improve student support
iii. An influential report showing that non-completion rates are significantly high is published
iv. The lack of a strategical basis is officially recognised
v. The HMI is created
vi. Data on student completion rates for further education are published
vii. A minor report showing that non-completion rates are significantly high is published

Questions 4–8

Complete the sentences below. Use **NO MORE THAN THREE WORDS** from the passage to fill each blank space.

Write your answers in Boxes 4 – 8 on your answer sheet.

4. Further education colleges in Britain were originally not worried about student drop-out, because students did not leave college for fear of ______________.

5. According to the writer, the philosophy at further education colleges was ______________.

6. As people became more aware of equal opportunities, colleges encouraged students from under-represented groups, as a move to ________________.

7. The HMI's report focused on completion rates, based on ________________ of reasons for students' departure from college.

8. In the early 1990s, the political situation, both in Britain and the US, demanded a drastic ________________.

Questions 9–14

Choose the appropriate letters **A** –**D** and write them in Boxes 9–14 on your answer sheet.

9. The report *Unfinished Business* ...

A pointed out the politics of the time
B gave £500 million to the state
C linked drop-out to wasting money
D turned the spotlight

10. The new series of principles developed in 1994 by the FEFC ...

A gave money to each student
B was quasi-independent
C meant colleges had to turn their immediate attention to improving student retention rates
D was aimed at improving teacher retention rates

11. Attempts to reduce the student drop-out rate were hindered, because ...

A there was a lack of research data on which to base strategies
B colleges did not know what to do
C computers in colleges were slow
D colleges had no patterns

12. Further hindrances in reducing the student drop-out rate were ...

A colleges' slowness in computerising data and not knowing their retention rates, nor what patterns of retention existed
B college inertia and administrative incompetence
C computer glitches and strikes, which occurred at most colleges
D colleges not knowing their retention rates or where the patterns were

13. Colleges' strategies to deal with the problem of low retention ...

A brought administrative and academic staff together
B varied enormously
C jumped
D were based on something other than data

14. The main strategies to improve retention included ...

A 'best fit' supporting activities
B activities to support and transform the student
C the raising of college expectations
D a summary by Martinez

Reading Passage 2

You should spend about 20 minutes on **Questions 15–27**, which are based on **Reading Passage 2** below.

Another intelligence?

Emotional intelligence as a theory was first brought to public attention by the book *Emotional Intelligence, Why It Can Matter More Than IQ* by Daniel Goleman, but the theory itself is, in fact, attributed to two Americans, John D Mayer and Peter Salovey. What is emotional intelligence exactly? According to Goleman, Emotional Intelligence consists of five key elements. The first is knowing one's own emotions: being able to recognise that one is in an emotional state and having the ability to identify which emotion is being experienced, even if it is not a particularly comfortable feeling to admit to, e.g. jealousy or envy.

Emotional awareness can then lead to managing one's emotions. This involves dealing with emotions, like jealousy, resentment, anger, etc, that one may have difficulty accepting by, perhaps, giving oneself comfort food, or doing nice things when one is feeling low. Many people do this instinctively by buying chocolate or treating themselves; others are able to wrap themselves in positive thoughts or 'mother themselves'. There are, of course, many people who are incapable of doing this, and so need to be taught. The third area is self-motivation. Our emotions can simultaneously empower and hinder us, so it is important to develop the ability to control them. Strategies can be learnt whereby emotions are set aside to be dealt with at a later date. For example, when dealing with the success or good fortune of others, it is better not to suppress any 'negative' emotion that arises. One just has to recognise it is there. And then one just needs to be extra careful when making decisions and not allow one's emotions to cloud the issue, by letting them dictate how one functions with that person. The separation of logic and emotion is not easy when dealing with people.

As social beings, we need to be able to deal with other people which brings us to the next item on Goleman's list, namely: recognising emotions in other people. This means, in effect, having or developing 'social radar', ie learning to read the weather systems around individuals or groups of people. Obviously, leading on from this is the ability to handle relationships. If we can recognise, understand and then deal with other people's emotions, we can function better both socially and professionally. Not being tangible, emotions are difficult to analyse and quantify, compounded by the fact that each area in the list above, does not operate in isolation. Each of us has misread a friend's or a colleague's behaviour to us and other people. The classic example is the shy person, categorised by some people as arrogant and distant and by others as lively and friendly and very personable. How can two different groups make a definitive analysis of someone that is so strikingly contradictory? And yet this happens on a daily basis in all our relationships–even to the point of misreading the behaviour of those close to us! In the work scenario, this can cost money. And so it makes economic sense for business to be aware of it and develop strategies for employing people and dealing with their employees.

All common sense you might say. Goleman himself has even suggested that emotional intelligence is just a new way of describing competence; what some people might call savior faire or savoir vivre. Part of the problem here is that society or some parts of society have forgotten that these skills ever existed and have found the need to re-invent them.

But the emergence of Emotional Intelligence as a theory suggests that the family situations and other social interactions where social skills were honed in the past are fast disappearing, so that people now sadly need to be re-skilled.

Questions 15–19

Choose one phrase **(A–I)** from the **List of phrases** to complete each **Key point** below. Write the appropriate letters **(A–I)** in Boxes 15–19 on your answer sheet.

The information in the completed sentences should be an accurate summary of the points made by the writer.

NB. There are more phrases **(A–I)** than sentences, so you will not need to use them all. You may use each phrase once only.

Key points

15. Knowing one's emotions …

16. One aspect of managing one's emotions …

17. Self-motivation …

18. The ability to recognise emotions in other people …

19. Handling relationships …

List of phrases

A empowers and hinders us
B means many people eat chocolate
C involves both recognition and identification
D is intangible
E is achieved by learning to control emotions
F is the key to better social and professional functioning
G is particularly comfortable
H is like having social radar
I is that some emotions are difficult to accept

Questions 20–26

Choose the appropriate letters **A–D** and write them in Boxes 20–26 on your answer sheet.

20. Emotional Intelligence as a theory …

A is attributed to Daniel Goleman
B was unheard of until the 1970s
C is attributed to Mayer and Salovey
D consists of at least five key areas

21. One way of controlling emotions is to …

A hinder them
B suppress the negative ones
C put them to the side to deal with later
D use both logic and emotion

22. As well as being intangible, the problem with emotions is that they …

A are difficult
B are difficult to qualify
C do not operate in isolation
D are compounded

23. Misreading the behaviour of others …

A is most common with those close to us
B is always expensive
C is a classic example
D happens on a daily basis

24. Employers need to …

    A save money
    B know about people's emotions
    C employ and deal with employees
    D work scenario

25. Goleman links Emotional Intelligence to …

    A competence
    B incompetence
    C happiness
    D common sense

26. The fact that the idea of Emotional Intelligence has emerged suggests that social interactions …

    A happen in the family
    B need to be re-skilled
    C are becoming less frequent
    D are honed

Question 27

Does the statement below agree with the information in **Reading Passage 2**?
In Box 27, write:

Yes if the statement agrees with the information in the passage
No if the statement contradicts the information in the passage
Not Given if there is no information about the statement in the passage

Example: John D Mayer and Peter Salovey wrote 'Emotional Intelligence, Why it can matter more than IQ'

Answer: No.

27. The author believes that the lack of Emotional Intelligence will lead to the disintegration of the family as a social unit.

Reading Passage 3

You should spend about 20 minutes on **Questions 28–40**, which are based on **Reading Passage 3** below.

Pronunciation and physiognomy

Imagine the scene: you are sitting on the tube and on gets someone you instinctively feel is American. To make sure you ask them the time, and are right, but how did you know?

When we say someone 'looks American', we take into consideration dress, mannerism and physical appearance. However, since the Americans do not constitute one single race, what exactly is meant by 'look'? In fact, one salient feature is a pronounced widening around the jaw, a well-documented phenomenon.

The writer Arthur Koestler once remarked that friends of his, whom he met thirty years after they emigrated to the United States, had acquired an 'American physiognomy', i.e. a broadened jaw, an appearance which is also prevalent in the indigenous population. An anthropologist friend of his attributed this to the increased use of the jaw musculature in American enunciation. This 'change of countenance' in immigrants had already been observed by the historian M. Fishberg in 1910.

To paraphrase the philosopher Emerson, certain national, social and religious groups, such as ageing actors, long-term convicts and celibate priests, to give just a few examples, develop a distinguishing 'look', which is not easily defined, but readily recognised. Their way of life affects their facial expression and physical features, giving the mistaken impression that these traits are of hereditary or 'racial' origin. All the factors mentioned above contribute, as well as heredity. But the question of appearance being affected by pronunciation, as in the case of American immigrants (including those from other English speaking countries) over the course of many years, is of great interest, and calls for further study into the science of voice production. This can only benefit those working in the field of speech therapy, elocution and the pronunciation of foreign languages, and help the student from a purely physiological point of view. Naturally, the numerous psychological and socio-linguistic factors that inhibit most adult learners of foreign languages from acquiring a 'good' pronunciation constitute a completely different and no less important issue that requires separate investigation.

The pronunciation of the various forms of English around the world today is affected by the voice being 'placed' in different parts of the mouth. We use our speech organs in certain ways to produce specific sounds, and these muscles have to practise to learn new phonemes. Non-Americans should look in the mirror while repeating 'I really never heard of poor reward for valour' with full use of the USA retroflex /r/ phoneme, and note what happens to their jawbones after three or four repetitions. Imagine the effect of these movements on the jaw muscles after twenty years! This phoneme is one of the most noticeable features of US English and one that non-Americans always exaggerate when mimicking the accent. Likewise, standard British RP is often parodied, and its whine of superiority mocked to the point of turning the end of one's nose up as much as possible. Not only does this enhance the 'performance', but also begs the question of whether this look is the origin of the expression 'stuck up'?

On a Birmingham bus once, a friend pointed to a fellow passenger and said, 'That man's Brummie accent is written all over his face.' This was from someone who would not normally make crass generalisations. The interesting thing would be to establish whether thin lips and a tense, prominent chin are a result of the way Midlands English is spoken, or its cause, or a mixture of both. Similarly, in the case of Liverpool one could ask whether the distinctive 'Scouse' accent was a reason for, or an effect of the frequency of high cheekbones in the local population.

When one 'learns' another accent, as in the theatre for example, voice coaches often resort to images to help their students acquire the distinctive sound of the target pronunciation. With 'Scouse', the mental aid employed is pushing your cheekbones up in a smile as high as they will go and imagining you've got a very slack mouth full of cotton wool. The sound seems to spring off the sides of your face–outwards and upwards. For a Belfast accent, one has to tighten the sides of the jaws until there is maximum tension, and speak opening the lips as little as possible. This gives rise to the well-known 'Ulster jaw' phenomenon. Learning Australian involves imagining the ordeals of the first westerners transported to the other side of the world. When exposed to the merciless glare and unremitting heat of the southern sun, we instinctively screw up our eyes and grimace for protection.

Has this contributed to an Australian 'look', and affected the way 'Aussies' speak English, or vice versa? It is a curious chicken and egg conundrum, but perhaps the answer is ultimately irrelevant. Of course other factors affect the way people look and sound, and I am not suggesting for one minute that all those who speak one form of a language or dialect have a set physiognomy because of their pronunciation patterns. But a large enough number do, and that alone is worth investigating. What is important, however, is establishing pronunciation as one of the factors that determine physiognomy, and gaining a deeper insight into the origins and nature of the sounds of speech. And of course, one wonders what 'look' one's own group has!

Questions 28–30

Use the information in the text to match the **People** listed **(28–30)** with the **Observations (i–vii)**. Write the appropriate letter in Boxes 28–30 on your answer sheet. Note that there are more **Observations** than **people,** so you will not use all of them. You can use each **Observation** once only.

People

28. Koestler
29. Fishberg
30. Emerson

Observations

i Americans use their jaw more to enunciate
ii Immigrants acquire physiognomical features common among the indigenous population
iii Facial expression and physical features are hereditary
iv Lifestyle affects physiognomy
v Americans have a broadened jaw
vi The appearance of his friends had changed since they moved to the United States
vii The change of countenance was unremarkable

Questions 31–36

Do the statements below agree with the information in **Reading Passage 3**? In Boxes 31–36, write:

Yes if the statement agrees with the information in the passage
No if the statement contradicts the information in the passage
Not Given if there is no information about the statement in the passage

Example: Appearance is affected by pronunciation.

Answer: Yes.

31. Further study into the science of voice production will cost considerable sums of money.

32. The psychological and socio-linguistic factors that make it difficult for adult learners of foreign languages to gain 'good' pronunciation are not as important as other factors.

33. Speech organs are muscles.

34. New phonemes are difficult to learn.

35. People often make fun of standard British RP.

36. Facial features contribute to the incomprehensibility of Midlands English.

Questions 37–40

Choose one phrase **(A–I)** from the **List of phrases** to complete each **Key point** below. Write the appropriate letters **(A–I)** in Boxes 37–40 on your answer sheet.

The information in the completed sentences should be an accurate summary of the points made by the writer.

NB. There are more phrases **(A–I)** than sentences, so you will not need to use them all. You may use each phrase once only.

Key points

37. Voice coaches ...

38. The Scouse accent ...

39. Whether the way we look affects the way we speak or the other way round ...

40. It is important to prove that pronunciation ...

List of phrases

A can be achieved by using a mental aid
B is irrelevant
C is worth investigating
D use images to assist students with the desired pronunciation
E is a chicken and egg conundrum
F get the target
G can affect appearance
H is not as easy as a Belfast one
I makes you smile

Test 5

Reading Passage 1

You should spend about 20 minutes on **Questions 1–14,** which are based on **Reading Passage 1** below.

Day after day we hear about how anthropogenic development is causing global warming. According to an increasingly vocal minority, however, we should be asking ourselves how much of this is media hype and how much is based on real evidence. It seems, as so often is the case, that it depends on which expert you listen to, or which statistics you study.

Yes, it is true that there is a mass of evidence to indicate that the world is getting warmer, with one of the world's leading weather predictors stating that air temperatures have shown an increase of just under half a degree Celsius since the beginning of the twentieth century. And while this may not sound like anything worth losing sleep over, the international press would have us believe that the consequences could be devastating. Other experts, however, are of the opinion that what we are seeing is just part of a natural upward and downward swing that has always been part of the cycle of global weather. An analysis of the views of major meteorologists in the United States showed that less than 20% of them believed that any change in temperature over the last hundred years was our own fault–the rest attributed it to natural cyclical changes.

There is, of course, no denying that we are still at a very early stage in understanding weather. The effects of such variables as rainfall, cloud formation, the seas and oceans, gases such as methane and ozone, or even solar energy are still not really understood, and therefore the predictions that we make using them cannot always be relied on. Dr. James Hansen, in 1988, was predicting that the likely effects of global warming would be a raising of world temperature which would have disastrous consequences for mankind: "a strong cause and effect relationship between the current climate and human alteration of the atmosphere". He has now gone on record as stating that using artificial models of climate as a way of predicting change is all but impossible. In fact, he now believes that, rather than getting hotter, our planet is getting greener as a result of the carbon dioxide increase, with the prospect of increasing vegetation in areas which in recent history have been frozen wastelands.

In fact, there is some evidence to suggest that as our computer-based weather models have become more sophisticated, the predicted rises in temperature have been cut back. In addition, if we look at the much reported rise in global temperature over the last century, a close analysis reveals that the lion's share of that increase, almost three quarters in total, occurred before man began to 'poison' his world with industrial processes and the accompanying greenhouse gas emissions in the second half of the twentieth century.

So should we pay any attention to those stories that scream out at us from billboards and television news headlines, claiming that man, with his inexhaustible dependence on oil-based machinery and ever more sophisticated forms of transport is creating a nightmare level of greenhouse gas emissions, poisoning his environment and ripping open the ozone layer? Doubters point to scientific evidence, which can prove that, of all the greenhouse gases, only two percent come from man-made sources, the rest resulting from natural emissions.

Who, then, to believe: the environmentalist exhorting us to leave the car at home, to buy re-usable products packaged in recycled paper and to plant trees in our back yard? Or the sceptics, including, of course, a lot of big businesses who have most to lose, when they tell us that we are making a mountain out of a molehill? And my own opinion? The jury's still out as far as I am concerned!

Questions 1–5

Choose the appropriate letters **A–D** and write them in Boxes 1–5 on your answer sheet.

1. The author ...

   A believes that man is causing global warming
   B believes that global warming is a natural process
   C is sure what the causes of global warming are
   D does not say what he believes the causes of global warming are

2. As to the cause of global warming, the author believes that ...

   A occasionally the facts depend on who you are talking to
   B the facts always depend on who you are talking to
   C often the facts depend on which expert you listen to
   D you should not speak to experts

3. More than 80% of the top meteorologists in the United States are of the opinion that ...

   A global warming should make us lose sleep
   B global warming is not the result of natural cyclical changes, but man-made
   C the consequences of global warming will be devastating
   D global warming is not man-made, but the result of natural cyclical changes

4. Our understanding of weather ...

   A leads to reliable predictions
   B is variable
   C cannot be denied
   D is not very developed yet

5. Currently, Dr James Hansen's beliefs include the fact that ...

   A it is nearly impossible to predict weather change using artificial models
   B the consequences of global warming would be disastrous for mankind
   C there is a significant link between the climate now, and man's changing of the atmosphere
   D Earth is getting colder

Questions 6–11

Do the statements below agree with the information in **Reading Passage 1**?
In Boxes 6–11, write:

Yes if the statement agrees with the information in the passage
No if the statement contradicts the information in the passage
Not Given if there is no information about the statement in the passage

Example: Computer-based weather models have become more sophisticated.

Answer: Yes.

6. At the same time that computer–based weather models have become more sophisticated, weather forecasters have become more expert.

7. Most of the increase in global temperature happened in the second half of the twentieth century.

8. The media wants us to blame ourselves for global warming.

9. The media encourages the public to use environmentally friendly vehicles, such as electric cars to combat global warming.

10. Environmentalists are very effective at persuading people to be kind to the environment.

11. Many big businesses are on the side of the sceptics as regards the cause of global warming.

Questions 12 and 13

Complete the sentences below. Use **NO MORE THAN THREE WORDS** from the passage for each blank space.

Write your answers in Boxes 12 and 13 on your answer sheet.

12. As well as planting trees and not driving, the environmentalist would like us to choose products that are wrapped _______________ and can be used more than once.

13. Big businesses would have us believe that we are making too much fuss about global warming, because they have _______________.

Question 14

Choose the appropriate letter **A–D** and write it in Box 14 on your answer sheet.

14. Which of these is the best title for this text?

A Global Warming is for real
B Global warming–media hype or genuine threat?
C Weather changes over the last 100 years
D Global Warming–the greatest threat to mankind

Reading Passage 2

You should spend about 20 minutes on **Questions 15–28,** which are based on **Reading Passage 2** below.

Questions 15–21

Reading Passage 2 has 8 paragraphs **(A–H)**. Choose the most suitable heading for each paragraph from the **List of headings** below. Write the appropriate numbers **(i–xiii)** in Boxes 15–21 on your answer sheet.

One of the headings has been done for you as an example.

NB. There are more headings than paragraphs, so you will not use all of them.

15. **Paragraph A**
16. **Paragraph B**
17. **Paragraph C**
18. **Paragraph D**
19. **Paragraph E**
20. **Paragraph F**
21. **Paragraph G**

Example **Paragraph H** Answer: x

List of headings

i. 165 million years
ii. The body plan of archosaurs
iii. Dinosaurs–terrible lizards
iv. Classification according to pelvic anatomy
v. The suborders of Saurischia
vi. Lizards and dinosaurs – two distinct superorders
vii. Unique body plan helps identify dinosaurs from other animals
viii. Herbivore dinosaurs
ix. Lepidosaurs
x. Frills and shelves
xi. The origins of dinosaurs and lizards
xii. Bird-hipped dinosaurs
xiii. Skull bones distinguish dinosaurs from other archosaurs

What is a dinosaur?

A. Although the name dinosaur is derived from the Greek for "terrible lizard", dinosaurs were not, in fact, lizards at all. Like lizards, dinosaurs are included in the class Reptilia, or reptiles, one of the five main classes of Vertebrata, animals with backbones. However, at the next level of classification, within reptiles, significant differences in the skeletal anatomy of lizards and dinosaurs have led scientists to place these groups of animals into two different superorders: Lepidosauria, or lepidosaurs, and Archosauria, or archosaurs.

B. Classified as lepidosaurs are lizards and snakes and their prehistoric ancestors. Included among the archosaurs, or "ruling reptiles", are prehistoric and modern crocodiles, and the now extinct thecodonts, pterosaurs and dinosaurs. Palaeontologists believe that both dinosaurs and crocodiles evolved, in the later years of the Triassic Period (c. 248-208 million years ago), from creatures called pseudosuchian thecodonts. Lizards, snakes and different types of thecodont are believed to have evolved earlier in the Triassic Period from reptiles known as eosuchians.

C. The most important skeletal differences between dinosaurs and other archosaurs are in the bones of the skull, pelvis and limbs. Dinosaur skulls are found in a great range of shapes and sizes, reflecting the different eating habits and lifestyles of a large and varied group of animals that dominated life on Earth for an extraordinary 165 million years. However, unlike the skulls of any other known animals, the skulls of dinosaurs had two long bones known as vomers. These bones extended on either side of the head, from the front of the snout to the level of the holes in the skull known as the antorbital fenestra, situated in front of the dinosaur's orbits or eyesockets.

D. All dinosaurs, whether large or small, quadrupedal or bipedal, fleet-footed or slow-moving, shared a common body plan. Identification of this plan makes it possible to differentiate dinosaurs from any other types of animal, even other archosaurs. Most significantly, in dinosaurs, the pelvis and femur had evolved so that the hind limbs were held vertically beneath the body, rather than sprawling out to the sides like the limbs of a lizard. The femur of a dinosaur had a sharply in-turned neck and a ball-shaped head, which slotted into a fully open acetabulum or hip socket. A supra-acetabular crest helped prevent dislocation of the femur. The position of the knee joint, aligned below the acetabulum, made it possible for the whole hind limb to swing backwards and forwards. This unique combination of features gave dinosaurs what is known as a "fully improved gait". Evolution of this highly efficient method of walking also developed in mammals, but among reptiles it occurred only in dinosaurs.

E. For the purpose of further classification, dinosaurs are divided into two orders: Saurischia, or saurischian dinosaurs, and Ornithischia, or ornithischian dinosaurs. This division is made on the basis of their pelvic anatomy. All dinosaurs had a pelvic girdle with each side comprised of three bones: the pubis, ilium and ischium. However, the orientation of these bones follows one of two patterns. In saurischian dinosaurs, also known as lizard-hipped dinosaurs, the pubis points forwards, as is usual in most types of reptile. By contrast, in ornithischian, or bird-hipped, dinosaurs, the pubis points backwards towards the rear of the animal, which is also true of birds.

F. Of the two orders of dinosaurs, the Saurischia was the larger and the first to evolve. It is divided into two suborders: Therapoda, or therapods, and Sauropodomorpha, or sauropodomorphs. The therapods, or "beast feet", were bipedal, predatory carnivores. They ranged in size from the mighty Tyrannosaurus rex, 12m long, 5.6m tall and weighing an estimated 6.4 tonnes, to the smallest known dinosaur, Compsognathus, a mere 1.4m long and estimated 3kg in weight when fully grown. The sauropodomorphs, or "lizard feet forms", included both bipedal and quadrupedal dinosaurs. Some sauropodomorphs were carnivorous or omnivorous but later species were typically herbivorous. They included some of the largest and best-known of all dinosaurs, such as Diplodocus, a huge quadruped with an elephant-like body, a long, thin tail and neck that gave it a total length of 27m, and a tiny head.

G. Ornithischian dinosaurs were bipedal or quadrupedal herbivores. They are now usually divided into three suborders: Ornithipoda, Thyreophora and Marginocephalia. The ornithopods, or "bird feet", both large and small, could walk or run on their long hind legs, balancing their body by holding their tails stiffly off the ground behind them. An example is Iguanodon, up to 9m long, 5m tall and weighing 4.5 tonnes. The thyreophorans, or "shield bearers", also known as armoured dinosaurs, were quadrupeds with rows of protective bony spikes, studs, or plates along their backs and tails. They included Stegosaurus, 9m long and weighing 2 tonnes.

H. The marginocephalians, or "margined heads", were bipedal or quadrupedal ornithischians with a deep bony frill or narrow shelf at the back of the skull. An example is Triceratops, a rhinoceros-like dinosaur, 9m long, weighing 5.4 tonnes and bearing a prominent neck frill and three large horns.

Questions 22–24

Complete the sentences below. Use **NO MORE THAN THREE WORDS** from the passage for each blank space.

Write your answers in Boxes 22 – 24 on your answer sheet.

22. Lizards and dinosaurs are classified into two different superorders because of the difference in their ________________.

23. In the Triassic period, ________________ evolved into thecodonts, for example, lizards and snakes

24. Dinosaur skulls differed from those of any other known animals because of the presence of vomers: ________________.

Questions 25–28

Choose one phrase **(A–H)** from the **List of features** to match with the **Dinosaurs** listed below. Write the appropriate letters **(A–H)** in Boxes 25–28 on your answer sheet.

The information in the completed sentences should be an accurate summary of the points made by the writer.

NB. There are more phrases **(A–H)** than sentences, so you will not need to use them all. You may use each phrase once only.

Dinosaurs

25. Dinosaurs differed from lizards, because ...

26. Saurischian and ornithischian dinosaurs ...

27. Unlike therapods, sauropodomorphs ...

28. Some dinosaurs used their tails to balance, others ...

List of features

A are both divided into two orders.
B the former had a 'fully improved gait'.
C were not usually very heavy.
D could walk or run on their back legs.
E their hind limbs sprawled out to the side.
F walked or ran on four legs, rather than two.
G both had a pelvic girdle comprising six bones.
H did not always eat meat.

Reading Passage 3

You should spend about 20 minutes on **Questions 29–40**, which are based on **Reading Passage 3** below.

Doesn't that sound terribly yellow to you?

'I can't say. I'm colour blind', was my flat-mate's response. And that was that for another twenty odd years, when by chance I came across an article in a newspaper on research into synaesthesia at a London hospital. At last, I understood my interpretation of the world through colour.

Synaesthesia is *the subjective sensation of a sense other than the one being stimulated.* For example, the sight of a word may evoke sensations of colour or the sound of music may also have a similar effect, as may taste. Or, to put it simply, synaesthetes, i.e. people with synaesthesia, have their senses hooked together, so that they experience several senses simultaneously.

To those not already aware of it, synaesthesia seems a new phenomenon. Yet, it is far from new. In 1690, John Locke, the philosopher, wrote of a blind man with synaesthetic capabilities. The first reference in the medical field was in 1710, by Thomas Woodhouse, an English ophthalmologist. In his *Theory of Colour*, the German writer, Goethe, talked about colour and the senses. The poet, Arthur Rimbaud, wrote about synaesthesia in his 1871 poem *Voyelles*, as did another French poet Baudelaire, in *Correspondance*. So, synaesthesia has a respectable history.

Synaesthesia is understandably met with a certain degree of scepticism, since it is something beyond the ken of the vast majority of people. *Son et lumière* shows in the 19th century were an attempt at combining the senses in a public display, but such displays were not capable of conveying the sensations experienced by *involuntary synaethesia*, as the ability which a synaesthete's experience is called. There has been a number of well-documented synaesthetes. Alexander Scriabin, the Russian composer, (1871-1915) tried to express his own synaesthetic abilities in his symphony *Prometheus, the Poem of Fire* (1922). And another Russian, Rimsky-Korsakov, noted the colour associations musical keys possessed. For example, Scriabin saw C major as red, while to Rimsky-Korsakov it was white. Arthur Bliss, an English composer, based his 1922 *Colour Symphony* on the concept of synaesthesia. He did not claim to be a synaesthete; his colour choices were arbitrary and the project an intellectual exercise.

In the field of the visual arts, probably the best known artist with synaesthetic capabilities is the Russian artist, Wassily Kandinsky (1866-1944), credited with being the founder of abstract painting. It is said he experienced 'sensory fusion' at a performance of Wagner's *Lohengrin*, with the music producing colours before his eyes. He did not see colours solely in terms of objects, but associated them with sounds. He even composed an opera, *Der Gelbe Klang* (The Yellow Sound), which was a mixture of colour, light, dance and sound.

For many people with synaesthesia, knowing that what they have been experiencing has both a name and a history and that they are among a number of notable *sufferers* is a revelation. Initially, they often feel that there is something wrong psychologically or mentally, or that everyone feels that way. Then they realise with a thud that other people do not. Suppression is an option, but unwittingly some people have managed to make use of the ability to their advantage. While the condition of synaestheia may hamper many people because of its disorienting effects, it can also open up a range of new skills. It is not unusual for people who have synaesthesia to be creative and imaginative. As many studies have shown, memory is based to some extent on association. Synaesthetes find they are able to remember certain things with great ease. The person who associates the shape of a word with colour is quite often able to remember a longer sequence of words; and the same goes for other areas where memory needs to be used.

But this condition like all gifts, has its drawbacks. Some people see words as colours; others even individual letters and syllables, so that a word becomes a kaleidoscope of colour. Beautiful though such a reading experience may be, synaesthesia can cause problems with both reading and writing. Reading can take longer, because one has to wade through all the colours, as well as the words! And, because the colour sequences as well as the words have to fit together, writing is then equally difficult.

Questions 29–32

Do the statements below agree with the information in Reading Passage 3?
In Boxes 29–32, write:

Yes if the statement agrees with the information in the passage
No if the statement contradicts the information in the passage
Not Given if there is no information about the statement in the passage

Example: The writer is colour blind.

Answer: No.

29. Synaesthetes experience several senses at the same time.

30. Newspaper articles and TV news reports about synaesthesia are appearing with monotonous regularity nowadays.

31. Mention of synaesthesia can be traced back to the 17th century.

32. It is strange that many people are sceptical about synaesthesia.

Questions 33–36

Choose the appropriate letters **A–D** and write them in Boxes 33–36 on your answer sheet.

33. *Son et lumière* shows ...

A attempted to combine public senses
B were frequent in the 19th century
C were both public and involuntary
D did not reproduce the experiences of synaesthetes

34. Both Alexander Scriabin and Rimsky-Korsakov ...

A wanted to have synaesthetic abilities
B created a lot of documents
C linked music to colour
D agreed with Bliss in 1922

35. The Russian artist, Wassily Kandinsky, ...

A performed Wagner's Lohengrin
B found abstract painting
C also composed music
D saw objects.

36. At first, 'sufferers' of synaesthesia believe that ...

A other people have similar experiences or there is something wrong with them
B they are a revelation
C they are psychologically or mentally superior
D they are unique

Questions 37–40

According to the reading passage, which of the following statements are true about synaesthetes?
Write the appropriate letters in Boxes 37–40 on your answer sheet.

A Some synaesthetes are disoriented by their abilities.
B Unusually, some synaesthetes have great creativity.
C Memory is heightened by synaesthesia.
D Synaesthetes have gifts and drawbacks.
E Some synaesthetes use their ability to help themselves.
F Their ability can be an obstacle to them.
G Some synaesthetes write in colour.

Test 6

Reading Passage 1

You should spend about 20 minutes on **Questions 1–14**, which are based on **Reading Passage 1** below.

PROPAGANDA – THE GOOD, THE BAD AND THE UGLY

Imagine for a moment that you are an impoverished citizen of ancient Egypt, hopefully hoeing the desert and wondering when it will bloom. Suddenly, a cloud of dust appears on the horizon which eventually resolves itself into a gallop of horses and chariots commanded by heavily armed soldiers followed, eventually, by a crocodile of exhausted slaves lugging building materials.

They all come to a halt outside your home and you make a strategic withdrawal indoors, from where you watch them through a slit in the wall. In an amazingly short time, the slaves build a 40-foot high obelisk which is then surrounded by a swarm of stonemasons. Then, when the work, whatever it is, has been completed, the entire company withdraws as quickly as it came.

Once the coast is clear, you creep outside to examine their handiwork. The obelisk is covered with carvings of soldiers, looking remarkably like those who have just left, engaged in countless victorious battles, decimating the countryside and gruesomely killing people who look remarkably like you. Prominently portrayed, surveying sphinx-like the carnage committed in his name, is the Pharaoh. You can't read, but you get the picture. You, in consort with your disaffected neighbours, had been contemplating, in rather desultory fashion, a small uprising. You change your mind in what is one of the earliest examples of the power of propaganda.

Of course, as is often the case with big ideas when they are in their infancy, the methods employed in ancient Egypt were far from subtle. But over subsequent centuries, the use of propaganda was conscientiously honed.

It was not until the First World War that propaganda made the quantum leap from the gentler arts of persuasion to become the tool of coercion. As Philip Taylor says in War and the Media: "Before 1914, it simply meant the means by which the proponent of a particular doctrine...propagated his beliefs among his audience...propaganda is simply a process of *persuasion*. As a concept, it is neutral and should be devoid of value judgements".

It is unlikely, at least in the West, that propaganda will ever be rehabilitated as a neutral concept. The very word is now so loaded with sinister connotations that it evokes an immediate and visceral sense of outrage. For the use of propaganda reached its apogee in the machinery of the Third Reich. Hitler and Goebbels between them elevated it to a black art of such diabolical power that it has been permanently discredited among those who witnessed its expression. Indeed in 1936 at Nuremberg, Hitler attributed his entire success to the workings of propaganda. He said: "Propaganda brought us to power, propaganda has since enabled us to remain in power, and propaganda will give us the means of conquering the world".

It is therefore unsurprising that Western governments and politicians are liable to perform the most extreme presentational acrobatics in their efforts to avoid the dreaded 'p' word being applied to any of their activities. They have developed impressive lexicons of euphemisms and doublespeak to distance themselves from any taint of it, real or imagined.

Inevitably, the media is alive to this hypersensitivity and the 'p' word has become a potent weapon in its arsenal. It is used pejoratively, with intent to discredit and wound, as governments are painfully aware. For propaganda is the spectre that haunts many a government-inspired media fest. It is the uninvited guest, the empty chair which serves to remind the hosts precisely why the gathering has been convened and forces them to run quality tests on the fare on offer – is it factually nutritious, is it presented in a balanced and truthful way, is its integrity intact?

In this one respect, at least, the negative connotations attached to propaganda actually perform a positive function. They offer a salutary reminder of all that government information is supposed not to be, and act as a ferocious curb on any runaway tendency to excess. Most importantly, the public is alive to the dangers of propaganda and alert to its manifestations whether overt or covert. They know that propaganda is the serpent lurking in the tree of knowledge; that it is subtle, it beguiles, it seduces, it obfuscates, it holds out simple dreams and turns them into nightmare realities, it subverts, it pretends to be other than it is. They know that it is the poisoned fruit of the goblin market, not the plain bread of truth that is the staple diet of information. And they will not tolerate it.

They succumb instead to the more blatant blandishments of advertising, which might be regarded as the wolf of propaganda, tamed and turned to domestic use. Safe in the knowledge that the wolf has been securely trussed by the rules and regulations of the Advertising Standards Authority, they knowingly consent to being had.

Questions 1–10

Complete the text below, which is a summary of **paragraphs 1–4.** Choose a suitable word from the text for each blank. Write your answers in Boxes 1–10 on your answer sheet.

You may use any word more than once.

Example:
PROPAGANDA – THE GOOD, THE BAD AND THE __________
Answer: Ugly.

_____1______ that you are a poor ______2______ living in ancient Egypt, when a band of soldiers accompanied by a ______3______ of slaves carrying building materials appears on the scene. While you are inside your house, the slaves erect an ______4______ and the whole company disappears. The ______5______ features figures like those soldiers who have just left engaged in victorious battles and, in a prominent position, the figure of the sphinx-like ______6______. After briefly considering an ______7______, you and the other inhabitants change your ______8______ in what is one of the earliest instances of the power of ______9______, albeit a not very ______10______ one.

Questions 11–14

Choose the appropriate letters **A–D** and write them in Boxes 11–14 on your answer sheet.

11. According to Philip Taylor, propaganda …

A is needed to propagate people's beliefs
B was a tool of coercion before 1914
C has always been a neutral force
D was merely a process of persuading people to do things prior to 1914

12. According to Philip Taylor, propaganda …

A is not a neutral concept
B is value loaded up until 1914
C is a neutral concept
D was a neutral concept up until 1914

13. Politicians in the West …

A will do anything to avoid using the word propaganda
B like using the word propaganda in the media
C do not dread the 'p' word
D are consummate acrobats

14. The public …

A are happy to be deceived by advertisers
B are deceived by advertisers
C are not deceived by advertisers
D respect the advertisers

Reading Passage 2

You should spend about 20 minutes on **Questions 15–28**. which are based on **Reading Passage 2** below.

The pursuit of knowledge

According to the great English lexicographer Samuel Johnson, *knowledge is of two kinds. We know a subject ourselves or we know where we can find information upon it* (Boswell Life vol. 2 p383 18 April 1775). In the information-driven world we now inhabit, the latter has assumed a much greater level of importance.

At the time of the European Renaissance, which spanned the fourteenth, fifteenth and sixteenth centuries, it was considered possible for the educated, well-read man, the so-called Renaissance man, to possess the sum total of human knowledge. Admittedly, the body of knowledge then available was restricted, being held firmly in check by several important factors: the paucity of books in circulation at that time; the difficulty of acquiring copies of the texts; the need to copy texts by hand; and the cost of doing so. The example of Lupus of Ferrieres' search for the *Ars rhetorica* of Fortunatus in the ninth century was repeated again and again throughout the Latin West until the momentous advent of printing in the middle of the fifteenth century. Printed books saw the end of some of the practical limitations placed on the spread of human knowledge. The first revolution in information technology had begun.

Renaissance man was rapidly left behind by this development; and, henceforth, it would be increasingly difficult for the educated man to cope with the expansion of knowledge that flowed through Europe via the medium of movable type.

In today's world, the scenario could hardly be more different. The most well-read individual, whom we could legitimately call *information man*, or *homo sciens*, would certainly be considerably more knowledgeable than Renaissance man. Yet, because of the ever-expanding increase in the sum total of human knowledge over the latter half of the last millennium, and the changes in the world of technology, easy access to information has reduced the stature of the educated individual. All that he can hope to be now is an expert in a narrow field, not the all-knowing polymath of yesteryear.

It is not surprising to see people overwhelmed by the unlimited stream of information. There is simply too much of it to assimilate, and it is difficult to know what to do with the data once it is received; which brings us back to Johnson's words. But we need to add another dimension to his dictum, one which was probably true in his time, but is even more pertinent today: *people need to be able to use the knowledge they acquire and not just know it or know where to find it.* Our deficiency in this regard is, perhaps, the most singular failure of the modern information age.

Acquisitiveness is a natural human instinct. Children collect cards of footballers, or whatever is the latest fad. Stamps, coins and books are targets for children and adult collectors alike, as their basic instincts are played upon and nurtured by market forces. The desire to gather knowledge is nothing new. What is astonishing, however, is the way in which people treat the knowledge once it has been collected. It is as if the collection were an end in itself; and herein lies the great deception. We have turned the world into a large machine of information, a veritable vortex into which we are all being inexorably sucked. People beaver away amassing raw data, labouring under the misapprehension that they are doing something worthwhile, when all that is really happening is the movement of information from one place to another. We should hardly be surprised that, as this becomes apparent, disillusionment and stress in the workplace are becoming sadly the all too common consequences.

The world is not really the richer for having the current wealth of knowledge at its fingertips. It is like standing amongst the wealth of the British Library, the Bibliothèque Nationale in Paris or other great libraries and not being able to read.

So what is to be done? Training in collecting and processing relevant information, followed by learning to collate, analyse and select or discard is the obvious solution. But there is such a dearth of people who know what to do that one remains pessimistic.

The pursuit of knowledge is sadly not all it is cracked up to be.

Questions 15–21

Complete the sentences below. Use **NO MORE THAN FOUR WORDS** from the passage to complete each blank space.

Write your answers in Boxes 15 – 21 on your answer sheet.

15. Samuel Johnson was an ____________________.

16. Renaissance man supposedly possessed all ____________________.

17. The spread of knowledge changed with the all important ____________________.

18. According to the writer, today's information man knows more than ____________________.

19. The standing of the modern educated man has been diminished by ____________________.

20. The polymath of the Renaissance is described as ____________________.

21. In today's world, people are weighed down by the endless ____________________.

Questions 22–25

Answer the questions below. Use **NO MORE THAN FOUR WORDS** from the passage for each answer.

Write your answers in Boxes 22 – 25 on your answer sheet.

22. How does the writer describe people's inability in the modern world to use the knowledge that they obtain?

23. What is the desire to collect things described as?

24. According to the author, what has the world turned into?

25. What are the consequences in the workplace of moving large amounts of raw data around?

Questions 26–28

Do the statements below agree with the information in **Reading Passage 1?**
In Boxes 26–28, write:

Yes if the statement agrees with the information in the passage
No if the statement contradicts the information in the passage
Not Given if there is no information about the statement in the passage

Example The European Renaissance spanned the 14th, 15th and 16th centuries.

Answer: Yes.

26. As the world has a wealth of knowledge within easy reach, it is now richer.
27. Knowledge processing courses will soon be obligatory for all library workers.
28. The author believes that the pursuit of knowledge is worthwhile.

Reading Passage 3

You should spend about 20 minutes on **Questions 29–40**, which are based on **Reading Passage 3** below.

Between the Inishowen peninsula, north west of Derry, and the Glens of Antrim, in the east beyond the Sperrin Mountains, is found some of Western Europe's most captivating and alluring landscape.

The Roe Valley Park, some 15 miles east of Derry is a prime example. The Park, like so many Celtic places, is steeped in history and legend. As the Roe trickles down through heather bogs in the Sperrin Mountains to the South, it is a river by the time it cuts through what was once called the 'garden of the soul'- in Celtic 'Gortenanima'.

The castle of O'Cahan once stood here and a number of houses which made up the town of Limavady. The town takes its name from the legend of a dog leaping into the river Roe carrying a message, or perhaps chasing a stag. This is a magical place, where the water traces its way through rock and woodland; at times, lingering in brooding pools of dark cool water under the shade of summer trees, and, at others, forming weirs and leads for water mills now long gone.

The Roe, like all rivers, is witness to history and change. To Mullagh Hill, on the west bank of the River Roe just outside the present day town of Limavady, St Columba came in 575 AD for the Convention of Drumceatt. The world is probably unaware that it knows something of Limavady; but the town is, in fact, renowned for Jane Ross's song *Danny Boy*, written to a tune once played by a tramp in the street.

Some 30 miles along the coast road from Limavady, one comes upon the forlorn, but imposing ruin of Dunluce Castle, which stands on a soft basalt outcrop, in defiance of the turbulent Atlantic lashing it on all sides. The jagged–toothed ruins sit proud on their rock top commanding the coastline to east and west. The only connection to the mainland is by a narrow bridge. Until the kitchen court fell into the sea in 1639 killing several servants, the castle was fully inhabited. In the next hundred years or so, the structure gradually fell into its present dramatic state of disrepair, stripped of its roofs by wind and weather and robbed by man of its carved stonework. Ruined and forlorn its aspect may be, yet, in the haunting Celtic twilight of the long summer evenings, it is redolent of another age, another dream.

A mile or so to the east of the castle lies Port na Spaniagh, where the Neapolitan Galleas, Girona, from the Spanish Armada went down one dark October night in 1588 on its way to Scotland. Of the 1500-odd men on board, nine survived.

Even further to the east, is the Giant's Causeway, a stunning coastline with strangely symmetrical columns of dark basalt–a beautiful geological wonder. Someone once said of the Causeway that it was worth seeing, but not worth going to see. That was in the days of horses and carriages, when travelling was difficult. But it is certainly well worth a visit. The last lingering moments of the twilight hours are the best time to savour the full power of the coastline's magic; the time when the place comes into its own. The tourists are gone and if you are very lucky you will be alone. It is not frightening, but there is a power in the place; tangible, yet inexplicable. The feeling is one of eeriness and longing, and of something missing, something not quite fulfilled; the loss of light and the promise of darkness; a time between two worlds. Once experienced, this feeling never leaves you: the longing haunts and pulls at you for the rest of your days.

Beyond the Causeway, connecting the mainland with an outcrop of rock jutting out of the turbulent Atlantic, is the Carrick-a -Rede Rope Bridge. Not a crossing for the faint-hearted. The Bridge swings above a chasm of rushing, foaming water that seeks to drag the unwary down, and away.

Questions 29–33

Choose one phrase **(A–E)** from the **List of places** to label the map below. Write the appropriate letters **(A–E)** in Boxes 29–33 on your answer sheet.

List of places

A. The Sperrin Mountains
B. Dunluce Castle
C. Inishowen
D. The Glens of Antrim
E. Limavady

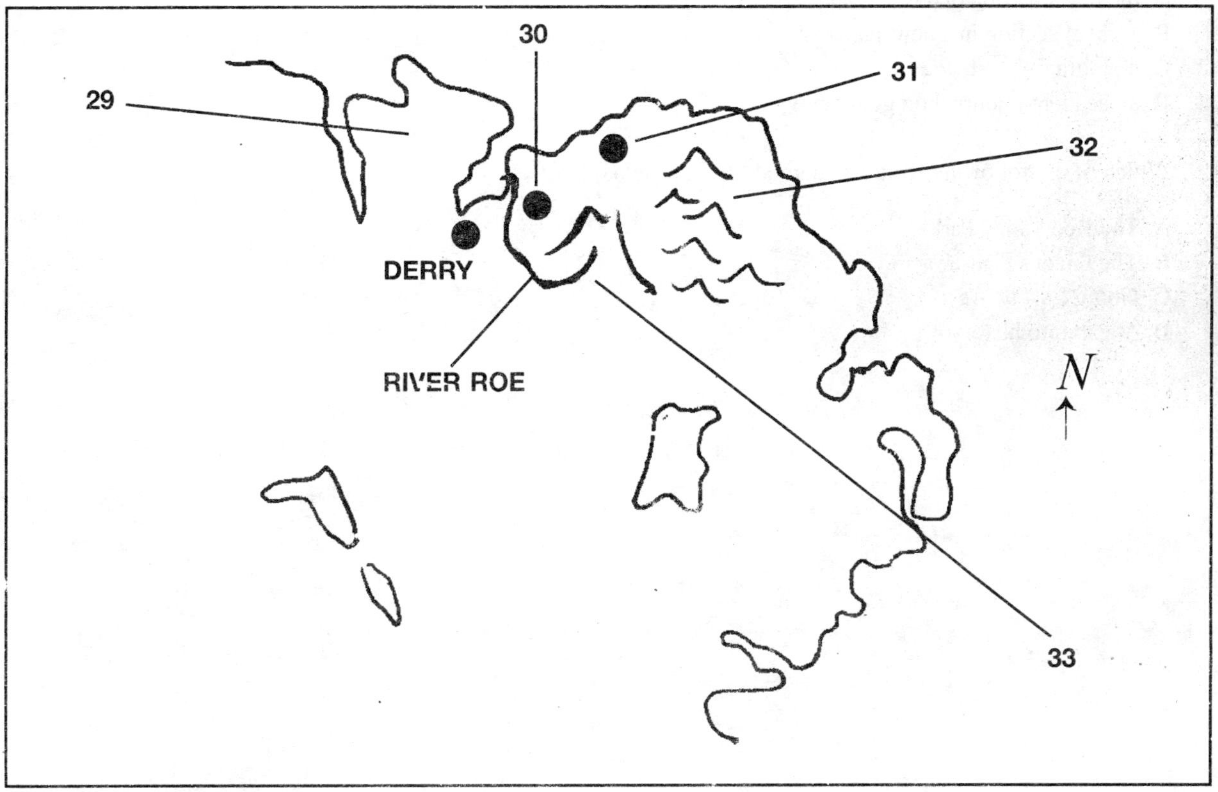

Questions 34–37

Do the statements below agree with the information in **Reading Passage 3**? In Boxes 34–37, write:

Yes if the statement agrees with the information in the passage
No if the statement contradicts the information in the passage
Not Given if there is no information about the statement in the passage

Example: Inishowen is in the north-west of Ireland.
Answer: Yes.

34. After 1639 the castle of Dunluce was not completely uninhabited.

35. For the author Dunluce castle evokes another period of history.

36. There were more than 1500 men on the Girona when it went down.

37. The writer disagrees with the viewpoint that the Giant's Causeway is not worth going to visit.

Questions 38–40

Choose the appropriate letters **A–D** and write them in Boxes 38–40 on your answer sheet.

38. The writer feels that the Giant's Causeway is …

A an unsettling place
B a relaxing place
C a boring place
D a place that helps one unwind

39. Where was this passage taken from?

A the news section of a newspaper
B a travel section in a newspaper
C a biography
D an academic journal on geography

40. Which of the following would be a good title for the passage?

A The Roe Valley Park
B The Giant's Causeway
C Going East to West
D A leap into history

Test 7

Reading Passage 1

You should spend about 20 minutes on **Questions 1–15**, which are based on **Reading Passage 1** below.

Lotte and Wytze Hellinga

A. As a student at the University of Amsterdam after the Second World War, Lotte found herself stimulated first by the teaching of Herman de la Fontaine Verwey and then by that of the forceful personality of Wytze Hellinga, at that time Professor of Dutch Philology at the University. Wytze Hellinga's teaching was grounded in the idea of situating what he taught in its context. Obliged to teach Gothic, for example, he tried to convey a sense of the language rooted in its own time and environment.

B. Study of the book was becoming increasingly important at the University of Amsterdam at this period, as the work of de la Fontaine Verwey and Gerrit Willem Ovink testifies. Wytze Hellinga's interests, formerly largely in a socio-linguistic direction, were now leaning more towards texts and to the book as the medium that carried written texts.

C. Much of Wytze's teaching followed his own research interests, as he developed his ideas around the sense that texts should properly be understood in the context of their method of production and dissemination. He was at this time increasingly turning to codicology and to the classic Anglo-Saxon model of bibliography in the realization that the plan to produce a proper critical edition of the works of Pieter Corneliszoon Hooft, the seventeenth-century poet, dramatist and historian, depended on the application of the skills of analytical bibliography.

D. Encouraged by his work, Lotte produced an undergraduate thesis on the printer's copy of the Otia of Constantijn Huygens (The Hague, 1625). This work, incidentally, has never been published, although an article was regularly announced as forthcoming in Quaerendo during the early 1970s.

E. On graduation in 1958, events took a turn that was to prove fateful. Lotte was awarded a postgraduate fellowship by the Nederlandse Organisatie voor Zuiver-Wetenschappelijk Onderzoek (or Z.W.O.), [illegible] to England to study fifteenth-century printing, and Marie Kronenberg, the doyenne of Dutch bibliographers, arranged for her to be "taught incunabulizing" (as she put it) by Victor Scholderer at the British Museum.

F. As an honorary Assistant Keeper at the Museum, then, she came to England in 1959, assisting among other things with the preparation of BMC volume IX (concerning the production of Holland and Belgium) while studying the texts of the Gouda printer Gerard Leeu to see if the sources (and hopefully printer's copy) for his editions could be identified. Although the subject proved difficult to define immediately so as to lead in a productive direction, most of this work was nonetheless to find its way into print in such collaborative publications as the Hellingas' Fifteenth century printing types, the edition of the Bradshaw correspondence and the 1973 Brussels catalogue, to each of which we shall return. But during her time at the Museum, Lotte's attention was also attracted by such things as English provenances on early-printed continental books, an interest which has stayed with her throughout her career.

G. Wytze's attention too was turning towards incunabula at this time, as witnessed by the fifteenth-century examples used in his Copy and Print in the Netherlands (1962), and there began a fruitful period of collaborative work which was issued in a stream of short bibliographical articles on Low Countries incunabula, and culminated triumphantly in the ground-breaking Fifteenth-Century Printing Types of the Low Countries, commissioned (at Wytze's instance) by Menno Hertzberger in 1961 and published in

1966. These years saw periods of intensive study in the libraries strongest in the incunabula of the Low Countries, with whole summers passed in Cambridge and Copenhagen as well as shorter visits to libraries from Oxford to Vienna.

H. The partnership between Lotte and Wytze was also to lead to marriage and to the birth of their son. Between 1961 and 1975, the Hellingas were in Amsterdam. In 1965, Lotte had obtained a research assistantship for Dutch prototypography from the Z.W.O., and from 1967 she was teaching at the Institute of Dutch Studies at the University of Amsterdam. She continued to develop her interest in analytical bibliography in a number of directions, perhaps most strikingly in important work on early Dutch printing and an examination of the Coster question. She also contributed to the catalogue which accompanied the exhibition held in Brussels in 1973 to commemorate the quincentenary of the introduction of printing to the Netherlands, a collaborative work that still provides the best presentation of the work of the early printers of the Low Countries.

I. The year 1974 saw the award of a doctorate by the University of Amsterdam for her thesis on the relationship between copy and print in a fifteenth-century printing-house, Methode en praktijk bij het zetten van boeken in de vijftiende eeuw. This seminal work, remaining as a Dutch dissertation of limited diffusion, has perhaps not been as widely read as it deserves. There followed a year's respite from teaching in 1975 with the commission from Ensched, to edit Harry Carter's translation of Charles Ensched,'s Type foundries in the Netherlands, at length published in 1978.

Questions 1–8

Reading Passage 1 has 9 paragraphs **(A–I)**. Choose the most suitable heading for each paragraph from the list of headings below. Write the appropriate numbers **(i–xv)** in Boxes 1–8 on your answer sheet. You may use each heading only once.

One of the headings has been done for you as an example.

NB. There are more headings than paragraphs, so you will not use all of them.

1. **Paragraph A**
2. **Paragraph B**
3. **Paragraph C**
4. **Paragraph D**
5. **Paragraph E**
6. **Paragraph F**
7. **Paragraph G**
8. **Paragraph H**

Example: Paragraph I: iii

List of headings

i. The classic Anglo-Saxon model
ii. Lotte to go to England
iii. More recognition deserved
iv. Wytze's research in Oxford
v. Wytze's interest in texts and the book
vi. Lotte unpublished
vii. Lotte to be published
viii. Lotte's first influences at university
ix. Lotte's work in England
x. The development of Wytze's research
xi. Back in Amsterdam
xii. A postgraduate student at university
xiii. A socio-linguistic direction
xiv. Wytze's interest in incunabula
xv. The birth of a son

Questions 9–14

Do the statements below agree with the information in **Reading Passage 1?**
In Boxes 9–14, write:

Yes if the statement agrees with the information in the passage
No if the statement contradicts the information in the passage
Not Given if there is no information about the statement in the passage

Example: At university, Lotte was first stimulated by the teaching of de la Fontaine Verwey.

Answer: Yes

9. Lotte studied at the University of Amsterdam after the Second World War.

10. Prior to his interests in the book, Wytze's interest was mainly in socio-linguistics.

11. According to Wytze Helinga, the production and dissemination of books were not really matters of importance.

12. When Lotte moved to England, she found it difficult to settle in initially.

13. Lotte lived and worked in Amsterdam during part of the 60s and 70s.

14. Lotte's post-graduate thesis was widely disseminated.

Question 15

Choose the appropriate letter **A–D** and write it in **Box 15** on your answer sheet.

15. The passage is an extract from a much larger text. What type of text is it?

A a biography
B a newspaper editorial
C a bibliography
D a travelogue

Reading Passage 2

You should spend about 20 minutes on **Questions 16–27**, which are based on **Reading Passage 2** below.

Party Labels in Mid-Eighteenth Century England

A. Until the late 1950s the Whig interpretation of English history in the eighteenth century prevailed. This was successfully challenged by Lewis Namier, who proposed, based on an analysis of the voting records of MPs from the 1760 intake following the accession to the throne of George III, that the accepted Whig/Tory division of politics did not hold. He believed that the political life of the period could be explained without these party labels, and that it was more accurate to characterise political division in terms of the Court versus Country.

B. An attempt was then made to use the same methodology to determine whether the same held for early eighteenth century politics. To Namier's chagrin this proved that at the end of Queen Anne's reign in 1714 voting in parliament was certainly based on party interest, and that Toryism and Whiggism were distinct and opposed political philosophies. Clearly, something momentous had occurred between 1714 and 1760 to apparently wipe out party ideology. The Namierite explanation is that the end of the Stuart dynasty on the death of Queen Anne and the beginning of the Hanoverian with the accession of George I radically altered the political climate.

C. The accession of George I to the throne in 1715 was not universally popular. He was German, spoke little English, and was only accepted because he promised to maintain the Anglican religion. Furthermore, for those Tory members of government under Anne, he was nemesis, for his enthronement finally broke the hereditary principle central to Tory philosophy, confirming the right of parliament to depose or select a monarch. Moreover, he was aware that leading Tories had been in constant communication with the Stuart court in exile, hoping to return the banished King James II. As a result, all Tories were expelled from government, some being forced to escape to France to avoid execution for treason.

D. The failure of the subsequent Jacobite rebellion of 1715, where certain Tory magnates tried to replace George with his cousin James, a Stuart, albeit a Catholic, was used by the Whig administration to identify the word 'Tory' with treason. This was compounded by the Septennial Act of 1716, limiting elections to once every seven years, which further entrenched the Whig's power base at the heart of government focussed around the crown. With the eradication of one of the fundamental tenets of their philosophy, alongside the systematic replacement of all Tory positions by Whig counterparts, Tory opposition was effectively annihilated. There was, however, a grouping of Whigs in parliament who were not part of the government.

E. The MPs now generally referred to as the 'Independent Whigs' inherently distrusted the power of the administration, dominated as it was by those called 'Court Whigs'. The Independent Whig was almost invariably a country gentleman, and thus resisted the growth in power of those whose wealth was being made on the embryonic stock market. For them the permanency of land meant patriotism, a direct interest in one's nation, whilst shares, easily transferable, could not be trusted. They saw their role as a check on the administration, a permanent guard against political corruption, the last line of defence of the mixed constitution of monarchy, aristocracy, and democracy. The reaction against the growing mercantile class was shared by the Tories, also generally landed country gentlemen. It is thus Namier's contention, and that of those who follow his work, that by the 1730s the Tories and the Independent Whigs had fused to form a Country opposition to the Court administration, thus explaining why voting records in 1760 do not follow standard party lines.

F. It must be recognised that this view is not universally espoused. Revisionist historians such as Linda Colley dispute that the Tory party was destroyed during this period, and assert the continuation of the Tories as a discrete and persistent group in opposition, allied to the Independent Whigs but separate. Colley's thesis is persuasive, as it is clear that some, at least, regarded themselves as Tories rather than Whigs. She is not so successful in proving the persistence either of party organisation beyond family connection, or of ideology, beyond tradition. Furthermore, while the terms 'Tory' and 'Whig' were used frequently in the political press, it was a device of the administration rather than the opposition. As Harris notes in his analysis of the 'Patriot' press of the 1740s, there is hardly any discernible difference between Tory and Whig opposition pamphlets, both preferring to describe themselves as the 'Country Interest', and attacking 'the Court'.

Questions 16–20

Reading Passage 2 has 6 paragraphs **(A–F)**. Choose the most suitable heading for each paragraph from the list of headings below. Write the appropriate numbers **(i–x)** in Boxes 16–20 on your answer sheet.

One of the headings has been done for you as an example.

NB. There are more headings than paragraphs, so you will not use all of them.

16. **Paragraph A**
17. **Paragraph B**
18. **Paragraph C**
19. **Paragraph D**
20. **Paragraph E**

Example Paragraph F Answer: iii

List of headings

i. The Whig/Tory division discounted
ii. Maintaining the Anglican religion
iii. The fusion theory challenged and supported
iv. The consequences of George 1's accession
v. The Tory landowners
vi. Political divisions in the early 1700s
vii. The failure of the Jacobean rebellion
viii. The Tory opposition effectively destroyed
ix. The fusion of the Independent Whigs and the Tory landowners
x. The Whig interpretation of history

Questions 21–27

Do the statements below agree with the information in **Reading Passage 2**?
In Boxes 21–27, write:

Yes if the statement agrees with the information in the passage
No if the statement contradicts the information in the passage
Not Given if there is no information about the statement in the passage

Example: Until the late 1950s the Whig interpretation of English history was the one that was widely accepted.

Answer: Yes.

21. According to Namier, political divisions in the mid 18th century were not related to party labels.

22. According to Namier, something happened between 1714 and 1760 to affect party ideology.

23. George 1 was not liked by everyone.

24. The Independent Whigs were all landowners with large estates.

25. Neither the Independent Whigs, nor the Tories trusted the mercantile classes.

26. Namier's views are supported by Colley.

27. Harris's analysis of the press of the 1740s is used by Namier to support his own views.

Reading Passage 3

You should spend about 20 minutes on **Questions 28–40**, which are based on **Reading Passage 3** below.

A. The medical profession is currently under siege as never before with a spate of high profile malpractice cases. This attack is taking place at a time when the National Health Service is undergoing a 'culture change' brought about by a shift in the public's attitudes to authority, in general, and, more specifically, by the demystification of medicine. The perception that doctors are a race apart is finally beginning to wane.

B. These forces have, fortunately, already led to a number of radical developments in the last five or six years in the way doctors are being trained, with greater emphasis now being laid on a more patient-oriented approach. Whilst, in the past, communicating effectively with patients was left basically to chance, this is no longer the case. As part of their final assessment, doctors now have to take a practical examination where their communication as well as clinical skills are carefully scrutinised.

C. If you ask most people what makes a good doctor, they will not say someone with sound medical knowledge. The first thing that will spring to mind is a good bedside manner; in other words, good communication skills. But what does a good bedside manner, or communication skills, entail?

D. All too often people complain about the lack of sensitivity of the doctors they encounter whether they be generalists or specialists. Some other frequently voiced criticisms are that doctors sound as if they are delivering a lecture when talking to patients; pontificating from on high. Or that they lack basic social skills; or indeed that they are bad listeners, concerned only with delivering their message rather than becoming involved with any kind of negotiation with the patient. So it would be safe to say that the most important aspect of a good bedside manner is good interpersonal skills.

E. From the patients' point of view, the interaction they have during their consultation with a doctor is very personal and hence emotional, while for the doctor it is merely a logical and objective process. And so, the chances of the doctor/patient communication breaking down are high if the doctor is not sufficiently skilled in handling the patient's emotional needs. A doctor must be able to deal with the full range of a patient's feelings, showing sympathy and empathy especially when handling difficult situations, like breaking bad news etc.

F. Another aspect of the good bedside manner, which is more often than not overlooked, is having the ability to talk to patients using lay language that they understand, while, at the same time, avoiding any hint of condescension, or being patronising. The inability to do this has a number of effects. When doctors use medical jargon, patients feel that they are trying to hide something. Doctors can also give the impression that they do not know what they are talking about; or even that they do not know the solution to a problem.

G. It is also essential that the doctor at all times is able to maintain authority. For example, doctors need to deal with some patients' belief that medicine is infallible, i.e. that the doctor has the panacea for every woe! This is certainly no easy task, as most people's expectations are raised by the daily diet of wondrous developments in medicine.

H. The other side of the coin is that, as people's awareness and knowledge have increased, albeit often misinformed by the internet etc, the stronger their doubts about the medical profession have become. And coupled with the rise in general educational awareness, the public have consequently a lower regard for doctors. This, in turn, has affected doctors' ability to communicate. They are not able to hide behind the veneer that technical jargon created.

I. At last, the pendulum has swung in the patient's direction. The onus is now upon doctors to adapt themselves to the patient's needs rather than the patient approaching some awesome god-like figure. The veil has been lifted and the temple violated.

Questions 28–35

Reading Passage 3 has 9 paragraphs **(A–I)**. Choose the most suitable heading for each paragraph from the list of headings below. Write the appropriate numbers **(i–xv)** in Boxes 28–36 on your answer sheet.

One of the headings has been done for you as an example.

NB. There are more headings than paragraphs, so you will not use all of them.

Example Paragraph A Answer: xv

28. **Paragraph B**
29. **Paragraph C**
30. **Paragraph D**
31. **Paragraph E**
32. **Paragraph F**
33. **Paragraph G**
34. **Paragraph H**
35. **Paragraph I**

List of headings

i. Still maintaining authority and patients' raised expectations
ii. Medicine mystified
iii. What makes a good doctor?
iv. The burden now on doctors
v. Good personal skills
vi. Good interpersonal skills
vii. The essence of medical training
viii. Emotion and logic
ix. Avoiding medical jargon
x. Doctors – born or made?
xi. Doctors' status lowered
xii. Changing attitudes effect changes in doctors' training
xiii. The swinging pendulum
xiv. Meeting patients
xv. A culture change in the National Health Service

Questions 36–40

Choose the appropriate letters **A–D** and write them in Boxes 36–40 on your answer sheet.

36. The change in people's attitude to authority has, in part, …

A mystified medicine
B improved medical training considerably
C affected people's feelings about authority
D effected a cultural change in the health service

37. Which of the following statements is true according to the information in the passage?

A Doctors need to be able to use lay language with patients and, at the same time, to avoid talking down to the patient
B Doctors do not need to be able to use lay language with patients, nor to avoid being condescending to the patient
C For doctors, the use of lay language with patients is not important
D For all medical personnel, the use of lay language with patients is important

38. How would you describe the writer's attitude to the changes in medical training?

A He is in two-minds about the changes
B He is against the changes
C He is luke-warm about the changes
D He is for the changes

39. Which of the following is the most suitable title for the passage?

A A change of emphasis in the doctor/patient relationship
B The patient's perspective
C An overview of medical training
D A panacea for all ills

40. The author wrote the passage ...

A to criticise the new developments in medicine
B to show how the public's shift in attitude to doctors has brought about changes in the doctor/patient relationship
C to show how the medical profession needs to be changed
D to blame the medical profession for society's ills

Test 8

Reading Passage 1

You should spend about 20 minutes on **Questions 1–14**, which are based on **Reading Passage 1** below.

This is very much the story of a story

The outline of the tale has been told before. It can be found in Edward Miller's history of the British Museum, Arundell Esdaile's book on the British Museum Library, rather more chattily, in Edward Edwards's Lives of the founders of the Museum, and most recently, and its first excursion this century outside the literature of the Museum, in Christopher Hibbert's new biography of George III.

The December 1850 issue of the *Quarterly Review* contains a long article reviewing a number of official reports into the functioning of the British Museum (including incidentally a review of the House of Commons Select Committee report of 1836, fifteen years earlier: it is never too late to review a good report. Although anonymous, it was written by Richard Ford, probably best remembered today as the author of Murray's *Handbook for travellers in Spain*.

The review contains much that is entertaining and amusing, and I must say it can be recommended today to anyone concerned with organising Library services, but for our purposes the bit that matters is the allegation that, among other things, George IV had been considering selling George III's library to the Tsar of Russia, until the British government intervened and arranged for its transfer instead to the British Museum.

This story was picked up during 1851 by a number of contributors to *Notes & Queries*, where various mischievous observations about what happened and who was involved were made. These comments revolved chiefly round the suggestion that the King's Library was not the munificent gift to the nation that it was claimed to be, but that the government had in effect had to buy the Library, either directly by purchase, or indirectly by agreeing to treat the King's requests for money more sympathetically than hitherto.

In August 1851, however, came a communication to *Notes & Queries* of a different kind from the previous notes, which are rather more gossipy in nature. It is signed "C." He writes: "I have delayed contradicting the stories told about the King's Library in the *Quarterly Review* of last December ... I am sorry to say still more gravely and circumstantially reproduced by the Editor of *Notes & Queries*. I have delayed, I say, until I w... enabled to satisfy myself more completely as to one of the allegations in your Note."

"C." goes on: "I can now venture to assure you that the whole story of the projected sale to Russia is absolutely unfounded". He then goes on to sketch in background about George IV's wish to dispose of the Library and the government's success in getting it to the British Museum.

"C." then objects in particular to the suggestion, made by the *Notes & Queries* editor rather than in the *Quarterly*, that Princess Lieven, the well-known socialite and friend of George IV's, whose husband was Russian ambassador in London at the time, had been involved in the plan. He explains that Princess Lieven was adamant that she had known of no such proposal, and therefore that that was that.

But that was not that. The December issue of *Notes & Queries* includes a short note, signed "Griffin", arguing that while Princess Lieven may claim to have known nothing, it did not mean that there had not been talk about a Russian purchase. "Griffin" also suggests that one of the King's motives for getting rid of the Library was to sort out problems arising from George III's Will (a suggestion, as has been pointed out before, that is incidentally supported by an entry from early 1823 in the journal of Charles Greville).

This provoked "C." to return to the matter in early 1852, when he argued that it was inconceivable that Princess Lieven would not have known that such a thing was in the air, given her court and social connections. In other words, the Russian connection is just idle speculation.

An interesting aspect of all this is that the initial stirring and rumour-mongering was all to do with money: was the library, or was it not, paid for? It is the intervention of "C." and his fervent denials that bring the Russians into prominence.

The identity of "C." is obscure. Arundell Esdaile identifies him as John Wilson Croker, the veteran politician and essayist. This seems to me unlikely: Croker was certainly involved in public affairs in the 1820s, but he was also a major contributor, a sort of editorial advisor, to the *Quarterly Review*, where the original offending article appeared. Indeed he wrote his own piece for it on the Museum in the December 1852 issue, without referring at all to the King's Library stories, and referring to Richard Ford's article in respectful not to say glowing terms. A footnote to his article, however, states that the *Quarterly* expected to publish an authoritative account of the King's Library business in the future: it never did.

Questions 1–6

Do the statements below agree with the information in **Reading Passage 1**?
In Boxes 1–6, write:

Yes if the statement agrees with the information in the passage
No if the statement contradicts the information in the passage
Not Given if there is no information about the statement in the passage

Example: The outline of the tale has been told before.

Answer: Yes.

1. The story that the writer is telling has only ever been carried in publications relating to the British Museum.
2. When published, the review of several reports on the workings of the British Museum in the *Quarterly Review* was anonymous.
3. The writer claims that it was Richard Ford who wrote the review of several reports on the workings of the British Museum in the *Quarterly Review*.
4. Richard Ford alleged that George IV was planning to sell his father's, i.e. George III's, library to the Tsar of Russia.
5. Murray wrote the *Handbook for travellers to Spain*.
6. The British Government bought George IV's father's library for a very large sum of money.

Questions 7 – 10

Complete the sentences below. Use **NO MORE THAN FOUR WORDS** from the passage to complete each blank space.

Write your answers in Boxes 7 – 10 on your answer sheet.

7. George IV's father's collection of books is known as the ______________.

8. Doubting that the collection was given to the nation, some commentators said it was not a ______________.

9. "C." says that the story about the sale of the books to Russia was ______________.

10. According to "C.", Princess Lieven was not ______________.

Questions 11–14

Choose the appropriate letters **A–D** and write them in Boxes 11–14 on your answer sheet.

11. 'Griffin' argued that the connection with Russia ...

 A could not be trusted
 B was genuine
 C was possible
 D was worth examining

12. Charles Greville ...

 A does not corroborate Griffin's suggestion that the sale of the Library was connected with George III's Will
 B partially supports Griffin's suggestion that the sale of the Library was connected with George III's Will
 C corroborates Griffin's suggestion that the sale of the Library was connected with George III's Will
 D was Prime Minister in the early 1820s

13. Which of the following is true according to the text?

 A The identity of "C." is obvious
 B The identity of "C." is not clear
 C The identity of "C." is Arundell Esdaille
 D The identity of "C." is John Wilson Croker

14. Croker ...

 A had been a politician for a long time
 B was an editor
 C was someone who advised politicians
 D was a minor contributor to *Notes & Queries*

Reading Passage 2

You should spend about 20 minutes on **Questions 15 – 27**, which are based on **Reading Passage 2** below.

De profundis clamavi*

A. But not too loud! According to the Royal National Institute for Deaf People, there has been a threefold increase in hearing loss and, in future, deafness will become an epidemic. It is hardly surprising that new research shows complaints about noise, in particular loud music and barking dogs, are on the increase. So dire has the situation become that the National Society for Clean Air and the Environment was even moved to designate 7 June 2000 as Noise Action Day.

B. There are so many different sources of noise competing for people's attention. Travelling on a train as it saunters gently through the countryside was once a civilised and enjoyable experience. That delight has all but disappeared. Because we have to reach our destination more quickly, the train hurtles at break-neck speed along tracks not designed to carry carriages at such high velocity. The train is noisier. And so are the occupants. They have to compete with the din of the train; and the conversations of their fellow travellers. And then there are the ubiquitous headphones (one set if you're lucky); not to mention that bane of all travellers, the mobile phone–not one's own, of course, because one has switched it off. The noise sensitive, a growing minority group, are hit by a double whammy here: the phone going off *and* the person answering in a loud voice, because they cannot believe the other person can hear. And let us not forget computer games making horrid noises given by parents to keep their children quiet! It is, however, gratifying to see that some train companies request people to keep the volume of their headphones down. It still strikes one as strange that people have to be reminded to do this. Like no-smoking carriages we should have more no-noise carriages: mobile-free, headphone-free, computer-free zones!

C. And the answer? Stay at home? No, not really. The neighbours do DIY: if you are lucky between 9 am and 7pm, and, if you are not, 24 hours a day. They play loud music, sing, play the piano, rip up their carpets; they jump up and down on bare floorboards to annoy you further. They have loud parties to irritate you and cats, dogs and children that jump onto bare wooden floors and make your heart stop. And, because they want to hear the music in other parts of their flat they pump up the volume, so that you can feel the noise as well as hear it. And if you are very fortunate, they attach the stereo to the walls above your settee, so that you can vibrate as well. Even if you live in a semi-detached or detached property, they will still get you.

D. People escape to the countryside and return to the urban environment. They cannot tolerate the noise–the tractors, the cars and the motorbikes ripping the air apart as they career along country roads. Then there are the country dirt-track rallies that destroy the tranquillity of country week-ends and holidays. And we mustn't forget the birds! Believe me, the dawn chorus is something to contend with. So, when you go to the countryside, make sure you take your industrial ear-muffs with you!

E. A quiet evening at the cinema, perhaps, or a restaurant? The former will have the latest all-round stereophonic eardrum-bursting sound system, with which they will try to deafen you. Film soundtracks register an average of 82 decibels with the climax of some films hitting as high as 120! And, in the restaurant, you will be waited on by waiters who have been taking their employers to court, because the noise in their working environment is way above the legal limits. Normal conversation registers at 60 decibels. But noise levels of up to 90 are frequent in today's restaurants. The danger level is considered to be any noise above 85 decibels! What is it doing to your eardrums then? Shopping is also out, because stereophonic sound systems have landed there, too.

De Profundis clamavi. The opening words in Latin of Psalm 130: Out of the depths (of despair), I have cried unto you (i.e. Lord).

F. Recently the law in the United Kingdom has been changed vis-à-vis noise, with stiffer penalties: fines, confiscation of stereo equipment and eviction for serious offences. Noise curfews could also be imposed in residential areas by enforcing restrictions on noise levels after certain times in the evenings. Tighter legislation is a step in the right direction. But there is no one solution to the problem, least of all recourse to the law; in fact, in some well-publicised cases, the legal and bureaucratic process has been unbearable enough to drive people to suicide.

G. The situation needs to be addressed from a variety of different angles simultaneously. There are practical solutions like using building materials in flats and houses that absorb sound: sound-proofing material is already used in recording studios and, whilst it is far from cheap to install, with research and mass sales, prices will come down. Designers have begun to realise that there is a place for soft furnishings in restaurants, like carpets, soft wall-coverings and cushions. As well as creating a relaxing ambiance, they absorb the noise.

H. Informal solutions like mediation are also frequently more effective than legislation. And the answer may partly be found in the wider social context. The issue is surely one of public awareness and of politeness, of respect for neighbours, of good manners, and also of citizenship; in effect, how individuals operate within a society and relate to each other. And, perhaps, we need to be taught once again to tolerate silence.

Questions 15–21

Reading Passage 2 has 8 paragraphs **(A–H)**. Choose the most suitable heading for each paragraph from the list of headings below. Write the appropriate numbers **(i–xiii)** in Boxes 15–21 on your answer sheet.

One of the headings has been done for you as an example.

NB. There are more headings than paragraphs, so you will not use all of them.

Example Paragraph A Answer: xiii

15. **Paragraph B**
16. **Paragraph C**
17. **Paragraph D**
18. **Paragraph E**
19. **Paragraph F**
20. **Paragraph G**
21. **Paragraph H**

List of headings

i. Social solutions
ii. The law backs noise
iii. Some practical solutions
iv. The beautiful countryside
v. Noise from mobiles
vi. Neighbour noise
vii. Noisy travellers
viii. Noise to entertain you
ix. Noisy restaurants
x. The law and noise
xi. Rural peace shattered
xii. A quiet evening at the restaurant
xiii. Noise on the increase

Questions 22–27

The passage contains a number of **solutions** for particular areas where noise is a problem. Match the **solutions (A–L)** to the problem areas **(22 – 27)**. If **no solution is given**, choose **A** as the answer. Write the appropriate letters **(A–L)** in Boxes 22–27 on your answer sheet.

NB. There are more **solutions (A–L)** than sentences, so you will not need to use them all. Except for **A**, you may use each solution once only.

22. Trains
23. Cinemas
24. Restaurants
25. Homes
26. Living in a rural setting
27. Shops

List of solutions

A. No solution given in the passage
B. People should be sent to prison
C. More sophisticated sound systems needed
D. Soft furnishings needed
E. People should stay at home
F. Sound-proofing materials should be used
G. Music should be turned down
H. The noise laws should be relaxed
I. Shops should have restricted opening hours
J. Trains should be sound-proofed
K. More noise-free carriages should be introduced on trains
L. Visitors should take industrial ear-muffs with them

Reading Passage 3

You should spend about 20 minutes on **Questions 28–40**, which are based on **Reading Passage 3** below.

Classical and modern

In the United Kingdom at university level, the decline in the study of Latin and Greek, the classics, has been reversed. As a result of renewed interest in reading classical literature and history, more and more students are enrolling on classical studies courses. The purists may deplore this development – 'it is yet another example of the 'dumbing down' of tertiary education with students studying classical literature and history in English rather than the original languages'. And, I must admit, they do have a point. But the situation is surely not as dire as the ultimate demise of classics as an intellectual discipline.

A classical education is a boon and should be encouraged. But, before looking at the advantages of studying the classics, which appear, incidentally, more indirect and less tangible than other disciplines, let us examine the criticisms that are often levelled against studying Latin and Greek.

The decline in the teaching of classics

The 60s with their trendy ideas in education are blamed for the steady decline in studying the classics. But the rot had set in much earlier, when Latin and Greek were no longer required for university entrance. With the introduction of the National Curriculum in secondary schools came the biggest blow. Schools came under pressure to devote more time to core subjects like English, mathematics, the sciences, history and geography. This left scant room for the more 'peripheral' subject areas like the classics. There was a further squeeze with the rush into teaching IT and computing skills. As schools could no longer choose what they wanted to teach, so subjects like the classics were further marginalised. Take Latin. In 1997, 11,694 pupils took Latin GCSE, while, in 1988, the number was 17,000. Comprehensive schools now supply 40% fewer Latin candidates, whereas grammar schools have seen a 20% decline. Latin candidates from Independent schools have fallen by only 5%. As a consequence, classics has been relegated to the 'better' grammar or comprehensive schools, and the minor and great public schools. Only one third of Latin GCSE entries come from the state sector. It can, therefore, be of no surprise to anyone when the pursuit of a classical education is attacked as elitist.

Tainted by this misconception, the classics are then further damned as being irrelevant in the modern world. Having been pushed into such a tight corner, it is difficult to fight free. A classical education is so unlike, say, business studies or accountancy where young people can go directly into a profession and find a job easily. For classicists, this is not an option. Other than teaching, there is no specific professional route after leaving university. And, with the pressure in the present climate to have a job, it is less easy than previously for young people to resist the pressure from the world outside academia, and from their families, to study something else that will make them money. The relevancy argument is a hard nut to crack.

The pertinence of a classical edcucation

Latin and Greek have been damned as dead languages that offer us nothing. The response to this criticism is, in fact, straightforward. Most European languages are a development of the classical continuum. And so having even a rudimentary knowledge prepares pupils for understanding other modern European languages. As for pertinence in the modern world, learning Latin and Greek are highly relevant. The study of these languages, develops analytical skills that have, to a large extent, been lost. They teach discipline and thinking and open up the whole of Western civilisation just as the discovery of the classical world did during the Renaissance.

Latin has also been called food for the brain. It gives students a grounding in the allusions in much of European literature and thought. Modern writers do not use these allusions themselves, first, because they do not know them, and, second, because their audience does not know them either. Sadly, most people no longer have the ability to interpret the allusions in art and the same has happened with the classics vis-à-vis literature.

The danger to Western and world culture is great if the classical tradition is lost. The spiral of decline is not just restricted to the United Kingdom. Other European countries face the same loss to their heritage. If we abandon the classics, we will not be able to interpret our past and to know where we have come from. A common refrain in modern society is the lack of thinking ability among even the best graduates. They enter work, perhaps as bright as any of their predecessors. But without the necessary skills they run around trying to reinvent the wheel. As Ecclesiastes says: *nihil novum sub sole est.*

But help is at hand. Concerned by the fact that fewer and fewer teenagers have access to a range of foreign languages, the government is harnessing the power of the Internet to introduce a distance-learning programme, where pupils will study Latin and other minority languages at their own pace. Initially piloted in 60 schools from autumn 2000, the internet-based courses will enable pupils to access advice from specialists by e-mail.

Questions 28 – 31

Do the statements below agree with the information in **Reading Passage 3?**
In Boxes 28–31, write:

Yes if the statement agrees with the information in the passage
No if the statement contradicts the information in the passage
Not Given if there is no information about the statement in the passage

Example: The decline in the study of Latin and Greek at university in the United Kingdom has been reversed.

Answer: Yes.

28. Fewer students are reading classical studies at university than before.

29. The purists welcome classical studies courses unreservedly.

30. The writer agrees fully with the purists' point of view.

31. A classical education is frowned upon in political circles.

Questions 32–40

Complete the text below, which is a summary of the writer's opinion on a classical education. Use **One Word Only** from the text to complete each blank space. Write your answers in Boxes 32–40 on your answer sheet.

You may use each word once only.

Example: Latin and Greek are known as the ____________.

Answer: classics.

The writer considers a classical education to be a __________32__________.

He believes that, in secondary school, the teaching of classics has been __________33__________ by the introduction of the National Curriculum. This has further led to the studying of the classics being attacked as __________34__________. In addition, studying Latin and Greek, is wrongly __________35__________ as being __________36__________, because classicists have no specific __________37__________ route to follow. As young people are pressurised to make money, the writer feels that the relevancy __________38__________ is difficult to counter.

In spite of the criticisms levelled at a classical education, the writer feels that learning Latin and Greek is highly __________39__________. And he fears that there is a danger that the classics as a discipline will be __________40__________. But help is at hand from a new Internet-based distance-learning programme being piloted in 60 schools from autumn 2000. The pilot study will allow pupils to study Latin at their own pace.

Test 9

Reading Passage 1

You should spend about 20 minutes on **Questions 1–10**, which are based on **Reading Passage 1** below.

Complementary medicine – an overview

A. The term 'alternative practitioner' first became common currency in the 1960s as part of a movement in healthcare which espoused a value system quite distinct from orthodox or western medicine. More recently, 'practitioners of complementary medicine' have sought to define themselves as distinct from 'alternative practitioners' in so far as they seek to work closely with the established medical profession to relieve a patient's symptoms. In a contemporary setting, the terms are often used interchangeably. But complementary medicine is perhaps a more fashionable term amongst those who aspire to greater integration within orthodox medicine–an attempt to gain respectability in the eyes of the establishment.

B. Complementary medicine comprises a range of physical therapies, including reflexology, aromatherapy, shiatsu and acupuncture, which can be used to help ease symptoms associated with a range of conditions. None of these therapies claims to be a panacea. They simply help to relieve symptoms, although in some cases they may result in a permanent cure. The basic principle is that the body ultimately heals itself with the intervention of a particular therapy 'kick starting' and, subsequently, speeding up this process. The therapies work on an energetic level to impact on a psychological, emotional and physiological level helping to alleviate short-term stress-induced conditions and, to a greater or lesser degree, chronic problems. All complementary therapies can be used as a preventative measure and to strengthen the constitution. Their common aim is to treat the whole person, with the goal of recovering the equilibrium between the physical, emotional and spiritual aspects of the individual. The focus is very much on improving overall well-being rather than the isolated treatment of specific symptoms. Where the therapies differ is their particular approach.

C. Reflexology is a treatment which was introduced to the West about 100 years ago, although it was practised in ancient Egypt, India and east Asia. It involves gently focused pressure on the feet to both diagnose and treat illness. A reflexologist may detect imbalances in the body on an energetic level through detecting tiny crystals on the feet. Treating these points can result in the release of blockages in other parts of the body. It has been found to be an especially useful treatment for sinus and upper respiratory tract conditions and poor lymphatic and cardiovascular circulation. Anecdotal evidence from various practitioners suggests it can also be effective in treating migraine, hormonal imbalances, digestive, circulatory and back problems.

D. Aromatherapy massage is a western medicine invention. The therapeutic effects of the essential oils used were first investigated early last century by a French chemist, René Maurice Gattefosse. Today, the beneficial effects of the oils are dispensed through aromatherapy massage, bath and shower preparations and the burning of oils. Essential oils work by entering the body through both the skin and lungs. Powerful molecules in the oils can affect cells in the nervous and circulatory systems to varying degrees. The effect on the olfactory centres of the brain is both physiological and psychological. Again, anecdotal evidence suggests aromatherapy is particularly useful in alleviating symptoms of respiratory illnesses such as bronchitis and asthma.

E. Shiatsu is a Japanese healing art deeply rooted in the philosophy and practices of Traditional Chinese Medicine (TCM). It is a hands-on therapy which aims to rebalance tensions and weaknesses in the body and mind. Shiatsu incorporates the traditional therapeutic massage of Japan, which in itself is an adaption of ancient Chinese massage therapy. Embracing its original focus of meditation and self-healing, shiatsu is gaining popularity in the West. The term shiatsu comes from Japanese: "shi" meaning finger, and "atsu" meaning pressure. In a shiatsu session, pressure is applied to various parts of the body which correspond with the points and energy lines (meridians) used in acupuncture.

F. Shiatsu has been successfully used for treating headaches, neck and upper back tension, lower back conditions such as lumbago and sciatica, other muscular-skeletal problems such as frozen shoulder, tennis and golfer's elbow, carpal tunnel syndrome, and osteo- and rheumatoid arthritis. Along with acupuncture, it can be very effective in treating digestive complaints involving organs from the stomach through to the large intestine and menstrual problems. It is ideal for people who have an aversion to needles or who prefer the hands on body contact that shiatsu involves.

G. Acupuncture is a very focused form of treatment which uses needles to rebalance the body's energetics. According to traditional Chinese philosophy, our health is dependent on the body's energy–known as *Qi* moving in a smooth and balanced way through the channels beneath the skin. Disruptions in this flow are associated with illness and pain, which may relate to anxiety, stress, anger, fear or grief, poor nutrition, weather conditions, hereditary factors, infections and other trauma. The insertion of needles into the skin and then energy channels helps to stimulate the body's own healing response and to restore its natural balance. Acupuncture has over 3000 years of empirical evidence to support its efficacy. It is probably the most effective way of treating a diverse range of conditions. These include conditions of a more emotional focus including anxiety states, depression (including what in the West is known as manic depression) , and sleep related disorders. Other illnesses treated by acupuncture include arthritis, asthma, circulatory problems (i.e high blood pressure, facial paralysis (pre- and post-stroke), fatigue, tinnitus, infertility, menstrual problems, rheumatism, multiple sclerosis, Parkinson's disease, migraines, sciatica, skin conditions and ulcers.

Questions 1–6

Reading Passage 1 has 7 paragraphs **(A–G)**. Choose the most suitable heading for each paragraph from the **List of headings** below. Write the appropriate numbers **(i–xiii)** in Boxes 1 – 6 on your answer sheet.

One of the headings has been done for you as an example.

NB. There are more headings than paragraphs, so you will not use all of them.

Example **Paragraph A** Answer: **viii**

1. **Paragraph B**
2. **Paragraph C**
3. **Paragraph D**
4. **Paragraph E**
5. **Paragraph F**
6. **Paragraph G**

List of headings

i. A panacea
ii. The René Maurice Gatefosse method
iii. Current practices in Egypt
iv. Therapy through the feet
v. Inserting needles into the bone
vi. Fingers versus needles
vii. Shiatsu explained
viii. Complementary medicine becomes part of the establishment
ix. Balancing the body's energy using needles
x. Treatment for digestive complaints
xi. Success with shiatsu
xii. An overview of complementary medicine
xiii. Treatment using essential oils

Questions 7 –10

Choose one phrase **(A – H)** from the **List of phrases** to complete each **Key piece of information about the four complementary therapies** mentioned in the passage. Write the appropriate letters **(A–H)** in Boxes 7–10 on your answer sheet.

NB. There are more phrases **(A–H)** than therapies, so you will not need to use them all. You may use each phrase once only.

Complementary therapies

7. Reflexology ...

8. Aromatherapy ...

9. Shiatsu ...

10. Acupuncture ...

List of phrases

A. is based on oils made from flower extracts
B. strives to rebalance tensions and weaknesses in the body
C. is based on several millennia of empirical evidence
D. has been found to be particularly useful in treating sinus problems
E. is based on ancient Chinese massage therapy adapted from ancient Japanese massage
F. is not very effective in treating migraine
G. is based purely on anecdotal evidence over thousands of years
H. is a form of treatment which affects centres connected with smell in the brain psychologically and physiologically

Reading Passage 2

You should spend about 20 minutes on **Questions 11–26**, which are based on **Reading Passage 2** below.

Testing Testing Testing 1 2 3 4....

The introduction of SATs

A. These are testing times. In both education and the field of work, the prevailing wisdom appears to be: if it moves, test it and if it doesn't, well, test it anyway. I say wisdom, but it has become rather an obsession. In addition to the current obstacles, like GCSEs, A-Levels, GNVQs, ONDs, and HNDs, not to mention the interviews and financial hurdles that school-leavers have to overcome in order to access higher education, students are facing the threat of 'new tests', *scholastic aptitude tests* (SATs).

B. SATs are being imported from the United States, where they have been in use for nearly a hundred years. As a supplement to A-levels, the tests purport to give students from poor backgrounds a better chance of entering university. SATs are intended to remove the huge social class bias that exists in British universities. But, in fact, they are, no more than an additional barrier for students. The tests, which masquerade as IQ tests, are probably less diagnostic of student potential than existing examinations, and, more seriously, are far from free of the bias that their supporters pretend.

C. First of all, as for any other tests, students will be able to take classes to cram for SATs, which again will advantage the better-off. At a recent conference of the Professional Association of Teachers, it was declared that school exams and tests are biased towards middle-class children. Further, the content of the tests in question is not based on sound scientific theory, merely on a pool of Multiple Choice Questions (MCQs), set by a group of item writers.

D. The questions in SATs are tested on a representative sample of children. Those which correlate with the school grades of the children are kept, and the rest discarded. This is highly unsatisfactory. There is also evidence that in MCQ tests women are at a disadvantage, because of the way they think, i.e. they can see a wider picture. And it is worth noting that MCQs are only as good as the people who write them; so, unless the writers are highly trained, those who are being tested are being judged against the narrow limitations of the item writers!

Other developments in testing

E. Globalisation has introduced greater flexibility into the workplace, but the educational system has not been so quick off the mark. But there are signs that times are a-changing. Previously, students took exams at the end of academic terms, or at fixed dates periodically throughout the year. Now, language examinations like the TOEFL, IELTS and the Pitman ESOL exams can be taken much more frequently. The IELTS examination, for example, is run at test centres throughout the world subject to demand. Where the demand is high, the test is held more frequently. At present, in London, it is possible for students to sit the exam about four times per week.

F. Flexible assessment like the IELTS has been mooted in other areas. It has been suggested that students may in future be able to walk into a public library or other public building and take an assessment test for a range of skills on a computer. The computer will dispense an instant assessment and a certificate. The beauty of this system is the convenience.

G. The workplace has been at the forefront of developing in-house schemes to establish whether people are suitable for particular jobs and/or careers. Psychological profiles and hand-writing analysis as well as aptitude tests are now part of the armory of the corporate personnel officer; an interview and a curriculum vitae no longer suffice. But, as in the education field, there are dangers here. Testing appears to confirm the notion that certain people are predestined to enter particular careers. All of us have heard someone say: he/she is a born actor, a born teacher, and so on. The recent work on the human genome and the research in genetics adds further credence to this notion.

H. How long before psychological profiling is introduced into schools to determine a child's future? With the aid of psychometric tests, children may soon be *helped to make more informed choices* about the subjects they choose to study at secondary school, and then university. But people will still be pointed in the wrong direction. In many cases, the result will conflict with the person's own desires, mainly because he/she filled in the test wrongly, or the test did not pick up an essential piece of information. Unless the assessors are highly trained experts, many more people will find themselves mid-life in jobs that they did not really want to do.

I. Whilst testing achievement is essential and indeed inevitable, it needs to be treated with caution. Tests are, after all, only tools – not an end in themselves.

Questions 11–18

Reading Passage 2 has 9 paragraphs **(A–I)**. Choose the most suitable heading for each paragraph from the **List of headings** below. Write the appropriate numbers **(i–xiv)** in Boxes 11 – 18 on your answer sheet.

One of the headings has been done for you as an example. Note that you may use any heading more than once.

NB. There are more headings than paragraphs, so you will not use all of them.

Example **Paragraph A** Answer: **xiii**

11. **Paragraph B**
12. **Paragraph C**
13. **Paragraph D**
14. **Paragraph E**
15. **Paragraph F**
16. **Paragraph G**
17. **Paragraph H**
18. **Paragraph I**

List of headings

i. Assessment in the future
ii. The theory behind MCQs
iii. Not enough testing
iv. Problems with SATs
v. Misuse of testing in schools
vi. The need for computer assessment
vii. The future of psychometric testing in schools
viii. Testing with caution
ix. Testing in the workplace
x. Globalisation in testing
xi. The benefits of SATs
xii. The shortcoming of MCQs
xiii. Too much testing
xiv. Flexibility in language testing

Questions 19 – 23

Answer the questions below. Write **NO MORE THAN THREE WORDS** from the passage for each answer.

Write your answers in Boxes 19 – 23 on your answer sheet.

19. What according to the writer has the present vogue for testing turned into?

20. Where do scholastic aptitude tests come from?

21. Who does the writer think SATs will benefit?

22. What is it that makes flexible assessment by computer attractive?

23. What has been at the forefront of developing testing schemes?

Questions 24 – 26

Do the statements below agree with the information in **Reading Passage 2**?
In Boxes 24–26, write:

Yes if the statement agrees with the information in the passage
No if the statement contradicts the information in the passage
Not Given if there is no information about the statement in the passage

Example: In the fields of education and work the prevailing wisdom seems to be to test everything.

Answer: Yes.

24. Research in genetics refutes the theory that people are predestined to follow certain careers.

25. Psychometric testing is favoured by headmasters and mistresses in many secondary schools.

26. The writer of the article is not in favour of testing in general.

Reading Passage 3

You should spend about 20 minutes on **Questions 27–40**, which are based on **Reading Passage 3** below.

Wittgenstein on Freud

Ludwig von Wittgenstein has justly been regarded as one of the major philosophers of the twentieth century, especially for his writings on the philosophy of language and logic. His work on psychoanalysis and criticism of his fellow Viennese, Sigmund Freud, have, however, been generally overlooked.

Wittgenstein is both highly critical of and at the same time greatly admiring of Freud's work. Perhaps it would be fairer to say that he is not critical so much of psychoanalysis as of Freud's claims for it. For Freud, it was essential that his work be regarded as science: that he had developed a new branch of medicine based on scientific principles, having established causal relationships between behaviour in childhood and that in adulthood. Wittgenstein, while accepting the usefulness of Freud's methods, disputes that these relationships are causal, therefore denying Freud's theories scientific validity.

In causal relationships we can at least imagine contradictory cases. For example, I can imagine placing a pan of water on a hot stone and the water freezing (of course I do not expect it to happen, and would be very surprised if it did). With Freud's theory, however, this is not the case. One of the central planks of this theory is the pursuit of hidden meanings in such things as dreams, works of art, even language (the famous 'Freudian slip'). Take the example of dreams. For Freud these are all sexual wish-fulfilments. While it is clear that some are, clearly some at least appear not to be. Freud, however, will not accept any contradiction to his theory, and argues that in these cases the sexual element is camouflaged, or even repressed. This is a strange notion, for how can a dream fulfil a wish if the desire is so disguised that the dreamer does not even recognise it? More importantly, if under no circumstances will Freud allow his hypothesis to be contradicted, how can we verify it? It therefore behoves us to recognise that, despite his assertions, Freud's theories are not causal hypotheses, and thus not scientific.

One might ask, given this analysis, how Freud came to make this mistake, or rather why he believed that his explanations were causal. It is a confusion between what we might call the 'depth-grammar' and the 'surface-grammar' of certain sentences. If we say 'the window broke because the stone hit it' we are outlining a causal relationship between the stone hitting the window and the window breaking, this being designated by the word 'because'. However, if we say 'he hit her because he was angry', whilst it may appear that the word 'because' performs the same function, this is not the case. The similarity lies only on the surface; if we look at the depth-grammar we see that in the first sentence 'because' denotes a causal relationship, whereas in the second we are rather talking in terms of motivations, reasons and other non-causal terms. Freud's mistake, therefore, is to believe that both types of sentence are similar: he confuses the surface-grammar.

Despite all this confusion, I have stated that Wittgenstein was highly appreciative of Freud's work, and this is because he essentially reformulates what Freud was trying to do. Freud believed that he was explaining people's behaviour, while Wittgenstein suggests that he is redescribing it. To him, Freud is providing a 'picture' of human behaviour which may enable us to make certain connections that other ways of looking would not reveal, and by showing these patterns and connections the method may well have therapeutic value. In this case, although the 'picture' described by Freud's method is not a true one (for by Wittgenstein's arguments it cannot be), nevertheless it is unique, enabling the patient to have insights into their problem that no other method could provide.

Questions 27–32

Do the statements below agree with the information in **Reading Passage 3**?
In Boxes 27–32, write:

Yes if the statement agrees with the information in the passage
No if the statement contradicts the information in the passage
Not Given if there is no information about the statement in the passage

Example: Wittgenstein was from Vienna.

Answer: **Yes.**

27. Wittgenstein was a great moral philosopher.

28. Wittgenstein owes the high regard in which he is held, in part, to his work on the philosophy of language and logic.

29. Wittgenstein totally admired Freud's work without any reservation.

30. Wittgenstein supports Freud's claims as to the causal relationship between childhood behaviour and that in adulthood.

31. Freud's theory on causal relationships enjoys considerable support in spite of Wittgenstein's objections.

32. The writer agrees with Wittgenstein that Freud's theory re causal hypotheses is not scientific.

Questions 33–40

Complete the text below. Use **One Word Only** from the passage for each blank space. Write your answers in Boxes 33–40 on your answer sheet.

You may use a word once only.

Example: The writer asks how Freud came to make this ___________.

Answer: Mistake.

Despite ____33______ confusion regarding surface-grammar, Wittgenstein held his work in high regard.

Freud believed that he was ______34_______ people's behaviour, while to Wittgenstein he was merely ______35______ it. In other words, Wittgenstein believes that Freud provides a ______36_______ of human behaviour, which allows us to look at things in different ways. This, according to Wittgenstein may be ______37______.

According to the writer, although Freud's 'picture' is not genuine, still it is ______38______. It allows the ______39______ to have ______40______ into his or her problems.

Test 10

Reading Passage 1

You should spend about 20 minutes on **Questions 1–16**, which are based on **Reading Passage 1** below.

A bad image not justified

'Flies are a nuisance, wasps are a pest...' as the children's rhyme goes. Indeed, local council environmental health departments everywhere recognise them as such. A wasps' nest in the vicinity of your home is certainly cause for concern. But all creatures have a function in life: flies *do* serve a useful purpose – they help dispose of waste matter and feed other animals higher up the food chain.

And wasps? To most of us they appear to possess no redeeming features whatsoever. Having been stung, the majority of people hate them and question their right to exist. As John Crompton points out in 'The Hunting Wasp', we generally tend to overreact to the presence of insects that are far more afraid of us, and whose only desire is to escape our company. Nevertheless, their sting is at least a nuisance factor, and, in the case of allergy sufferers, a serious health hazard, but wasps do not attack without good (in their opinion) reason. Very often, we accidentally disturb them, only to pay the painful price.

The problem is that two or three species give the rest a bad name. *Vespula vulgaris* and *vespula germanica*, the Common and German wasps respectively, are attracted to our food, and can ruin a picnic by challenging our every lick of ice cream, bite of sandwich and sip of drink. Barbecues are another regular battlefield, as wasps love sucking the juices out of meat. They also frequent dustbins and other unhygienic places, and so can pose a health risk, albeit not as much as flies. Another of their vices, often overlooked, is that they are fond of feeding mashed honeybee flesh to their young, while gorging themselves on the honey. Apiarists loathe them, for their raids seriously disrupt the normal routine of the hives.

This is not a complete picture, however, and it is necessary to redress the balance in favour of our black and yellow chums, notwithstanding the downside of course!

Together with bees and ants, wasps form the insect order hymenoptera, and can be divided into two main categories: solitary and social. The former need not concern us here, as they cause us no problems. They live alone or in small groups, and use their delicate sting exclusively to paralyse prey for their larvae to devour alive and fresh. They can also be employed in natural pest control operations. Social wasps are so called because they form large colonies of infertile female 'workers' ruled by a single queen. In Britain, apart from the species mentioned above, there are also the Tree, Norwegian, Saxon, Red and Cuckoo wasps, plus the hornets, which rarely come into contact with us.

There is also, of course, the *dolichovespula media*, or Median Wasp. Since it first established itself in Kent in 1985, it has spread rapidly throughout the country, provoking the tabloid press to dub it every year the 'French Killer Wasp' or the 'Eurowasp', blaming global warming for the superbug invasion! Indeed, it is larger than our native wasps, and its sting more powerful, but it is no more aggressive, despite what one reads in the paper. It will not bother you if you leave it alone, the point being that the sting of all social wasps is defensive, and will be used against anyone or thing perceived as a threat to themselves or their nest. Whatever is contained in that unlovely cocktail they inject is their secret recipe which scientists have still to analyse.

The life cycle of social wasps begins on a warm day in April, when queens emerge from hibernation and select a place for their nest, usually a hole in the ground, in a tree or in our attics, lofts and under our eaves. The structure is made from chewed up wood mixed with saliva, which forms a grey papery substance. The queen builds a dozen or so hexagonal cells and lays the first of up to thirty thousand eggs. The grubs hatch and she feeds them until they pupate. When the new adults, or *imagines*, appear about eight weeks later, the queen continues to lay eggs while her infertile daughters continue to build the expanding nest and feed the new larvae. In August males and females hatch, bigger and more brightly coloured than the worker 'caste'. Males, who have slightly longer antennae, are stingless, and can be seen in autumn mating with the young queens and sipping nectar from ivy, the last plant in Britain to blossom. As the weather gets colder and the flowers disappear, the males and the surviving workers die. The old queen perishes too, together with the last remaining untended grubs. Heavy November rains finally destroy the nest, although in milder climatic conditions colonies are known to last much longer. Having fed well to build up their fat reserves for the long hard winter to come, the impregnated queens seek out a suitable sheltered spot for hibernation, such as under a fold of bark.

We must ask those who would be rid of wasps what the world would be like without them. Quite simply, there would be far fewer flowers and much less fruit, and also many more flies, mosquitoes and other bugs, for they pollinate the former and favour the latter as baby food. So perhaps we should be thankful for these services, even though they come at a slight cost.

If we leave wasps alone, they will not hurt us. Just as we treat bees with caution and respect, so we should deal with wasps. They are fascinating creatures, which really *do* have the right to exist as part of our ecosystem, and besides being attractive, are actually beneficial in more ways than one.

Questions 1–4

Using **NO MORE THAN THREE WORDS** from the passage, answer the questions below. Write your answers in Boxes 1 – 4 on your answer sheet.

1. To most people, what do wasps not seem to have?

2. What do people usually do when confronted with insects which have a greater fear of people?

3. What do several species of wasp give other wasps?

4. What does the writer want to do as regards the image of wasps?

Questions 5 – 10

Complete the notes below. Use **NO MORE THAN TWO WORDS** from the passage to complete each blank space in the diagram.

Write your answers in Boxes 5 – 10 on your answer sheet.

The ____5______
Hymenoptera

Solitary

- cause no ____6______
- sting used to paralyse prey
- wasps used in ____7______ programmes

Social

- create large colonies of infertile female workers under a ____8______
- different species, e.g. Tree, Saxon, Cuckoo and Median wasp

- established in Kent in 1985
- known as Eurowasp
- larger than native wasps
- more powerful sting
- not any more ____9_____ than the native wasp
- sting is ____10_____, unless provoked

Questions 11–16

Use **NO MORE THAN ONE WORD** from the passage to complete each blank space in the summary about the life cycle of social wasps.

Write your answers in Boxes 11 – 16 on your answer sheet.

The life cycle of social wasps begins on a warm day in April ...

- Queens ______ **11**______ from hibernation.

↓

- each lays the first of up to thirty thousand eggs.

↓

- the ______ **12**______ hatch.

↓

- the queen feeds them until they pupate.

↓

- *imagines*, appear about eight weeks later.

↓

- the queen's infertile daughters build the expanding nest and feed the new ______ **13**______.

↓

- in August, males and females hatch.

↓

- the males ______ **14**______ with the young queens.

↓

- As the weather gets colder, the males and the remaining workers die.

↓

- the old queen ______ **15**______.

↓

- the impregnated queens seek out a suitable spot for ______ 16______.

Reading Passage 2

You should spend about 20 minutes on **Questions 17–27**, which are based on **Reading Passage 2** below.

Digital screams

A. What holds new advances in technology back is not the pace of development. Is it then the fact that people are generally conservative by nature? Or is it instead the inability of the marketplace to absorb new products fast enough?

B. There is always a time lag between new inventions and discoveries being made and the release of any related technology into the public domain. Like aircraft hovering to land at a busy airport, new products are frequently held in abeyance, while the marketplace is emptied of the last 'latest' gadget. Meanwhile, the general population are drip-fed information about what is to come. In this way, the public appetiite for new products is constantly being whetted.

C. People's blind faith in any new technological device prevents them from thinking through the implications of what is happening. Fewer and fewer people seem to have any serious misgivings about mankind's Promethean march to some great dystopia. Any lurking dangers are brushed aside, as are the diminishing band of dissenters.

... utopia ...

D. People are oblivious of the creeping advance of robots into their lives. Operations are being performed with voice-operated robots, not only giving surgeons an extra pair of safe hands, but also allowing a range of procedures to be carried out anywhere in the world by computer. Apart from surgery, voice-operated devices are also being introduced into cars. Drivers will soon be able to bark at mobile-phone-like gadgets cabable of supplying them with all the information they need from weather forecasts to stock market quotations. Who needs friends?

... a nightmare ...

E. Experiments have already been carried out on inserting micro-chips under the human skin so that people can be monitored at any time. Tagging is currently in use in some areas for criminals in the community. And data-tagging is being used for technical equipment like expensive motorbike parts and also for tracing lost dogs. Details about using micro-chips in humans have already been flagged in the press. And given the right circumstances, the procedure will be introduced with barely a whimper. Micro-chip implants might perhaps become the passport of the future.

F. Without out knowing it, you are already being monitored without the slightest hint of protest. The technology in your mobile phones allows you to be located. It is ironic that when mobile phones were first introduced they were perceived as status symbols. But now they are viewed as symbols of slavery, as bosses can monitor their work-force when they are out on the job. Video cameras in public places are now so wide-spread that it is possible to trace you for quite a distance. Supermarket loyalty cards and bank cards leave traces of your life everywhere.

G. As we naively come to accept the role of machines, they are appearing in roles that were exclusively the preserve of humans. Robots in bars already exist; soon they will replace hosts on chat-shows, and people as shop assistants or drivers and humans in many other professions. No? Do you take money from a teller at your bank or do you receive it from a robot built into a wall?

H. And much to the chagrin of traditionalists, toys have now come on the market which teach children to speak and which children can then communicate with. The novelty apart, this is a rather sinister turn of events. It is bad enough for adults to talk to cars and computers. But this development is much more disturbing. Children may develop certain linguistic skills from the robotic toy, but will lose out on the necessary social and emotional interaction. Social de-skilling of this kind will lead to untold social problems.

... or just a dream too far?

I. Yet, not all the developments are bad. The advances taking place in medicine, herald a new dawn for the human race. Disease will become an irritation rather than the bane it is now. Humans will replace body-parts as they wear out, with specially grown prostheses or electronic parts, whatever is in vogue at the time. Certain diseases which required huge resources and expenditure will be treated by gene therapy. Paralysis will become a thing of the past. By 2020, the life expectancy for new babies will be well over 100 years and more. Recently, the 'immortality' gene was located; so soon the world may be full of Methuselahs.

J. A nightmare scenario perhaps. Not half as nightmarish as the future possibility of downloading the human mind before the body dies. But I for one do not wish to live out eternity as some sort of digital collectable item. Against the hum of machines who will hear my screams? Or yours?

Questions 17–24

Reading Passage 2 has 10 paragraphs **(A–J)**. Choose the most suitable heading for each paragraph from the **List of headings** below. Write the appropriate numbers **(i–xvii)** in Boxes 17–24 on your answer sheet.

Two of the headings have been done for you as examples.

NB. There are more headings than paragraphs, so you will not use all of them.

Example Paragraph A Answer: xvii

17. **Paragraph B**
18. **Paragraph C**
19. **Paragraph D**
20. **Paragraph E**
21. **Paragraph F**
22. **Paragraph G**
23. **Paragraph H**
24. **Paragraph I**

Example: Paragraph J Answer: vii

List of headings

i. The time lag theory explained
ii. Humans helping robots
iii. A sinister side
iv. People are already being monitored
v. A novelty apart
vi. The dangers ignored
vii. A personal nightmare
viii. Some Methuselahs
ix. Robots helping humans
x. Tagging
xi. Hovering aircraft
xii. Technology not all negative
xiii. Drip feeding the public
xiv. Robots replacing humans
xv. Expensive motorbike parts
xvi. Who needs friends?
xvii. What stops technology from advancing faster?

Questions 25 – 27

Do the statements below agree with the information in **Reading Passage 2**?
In Boxes 25–27, write:

Yes if the statement agrees with the information in the passage
No if the statement contradicts the information in the passage
Not Given if there is no information about the statement in the passage

Example: There is always a time lag between new inventions being made and their release into the public domain.

Answer: Yes.

25. The writer feels that the general public have too much faith in the technological devices being introduced into the marketplace.

26. Tagging criminals by inserting microchips into their bodies will dramatically reduce the number of crimes being committed.

27. The writer of the article does not have serious doubts about the direction technology is taking.

Reading Passage 3

You should spend about 20 minutes on **Questions 28–40**, which are based on **Reading Passage 3** below.

Russian icons

The ambivalence of the Soviet authorities towards the art and artefacts of the Orthodox Church throughout the 50s and 60s is even more apparent in relation to icons. These religious paintings have always held a personal spiritual significance for believers in Russia, and some have been the objects of public veneration at a local or even national level. Conscious of the need to instil a sense of pride in the richness of pre-revolutionary Russian heritage, but wary of allowing religious sentiment to flourish, Soviet art historians strove to emphasise the uniqueness of the Russian icon tradition and its central role in the cultural development of 12th to 16th century Russia, while minimising its Orthodox Christian essence. It was a narrow path to tread.

One obvious ploy was to detach the icons from their normal setting in churches and cathedrals and display them in secular art galleries. This is particularly clear in the case of the Tretyakov Art Gallery in Moscow which houses many of the oldest, most beautiful and most venerated icons. Hung on impassive cream walls, these wonderful paintings are stripped of their religious significance encouraging the spectator to concentrate on their artistic merits. Elsewhere in the gallery hang the mordant social commentaries of nineteenth century Russian realist painters such as Repin, Makovsky and Yaroshenko, some of them specifically attacking the veniality and corruption of the Russian Orthodox Church, or mocking the superstitious ignorance of the Russian peasants. Further on are the paintings of the Soviet era, explicitly socialist, concentrating on human, particularly collective human, achievement. The peasants, now liberated from their attachment to religion and superstition (the two are synonymous in Soviet parlance), become heroic figures, contributing to the socialist future. The inference is not hard to draw: the icons belong to a continuous tradition of Russian artistic creativity which emphasises the dignity and universal emotional, intellectual and spiritual integrity of man, without reference to an external God. The Soviet authorities, of course, were not content to let visitors to the gallery draw this inference for themselves. It was explicitly stated in all the official guidebooks.

A further development in this separation of icons from their religious context can be seen in the creation of the Museum of Iconography in north-west Moscow. Housed in the former Andronikov Monastery, and named after the 15th century icon painter Andrei Rublev, the museum contains a representative selection of icons mainly from the 15th to the 17th century from various parts of Russia. The paintings are displayed in 15th century monastic buildings retaining the outward semblance of a church with monks' living quarters, but which have been stripped of all religious purpose. The guidebook stresses the harmonious lines of the museum buildings as if the original architects had designed them with that future purpose in mind.

Icons depicting the Virgin and Child lent themselves easily to appropriation by the secularising art historians. The Virgin is no longer the Mother of God, but a symbol of human motherhood, her sorrowing face no longer a foreboding of the death of her son on the cross, but an expression of universal maternal tenderness and pity. Icons of saints of the early eastern and Russian churches, such as St.Nicholas, Sts. Cosmas and Damian, and St. Sergius of Radonezh are similarly described in terms of their civilising influence, the humanitarian acts they performed or the role they played in the early development of a Russian national identity. Some of these saints were martyrs, dying for their faith, and so become symbols of Russian stoicism and steadfastness in the face of the invader. But icons of a more abstract or mystical nature, particularly those depicting the Holy Trinity, presented a more intractable interpretative problem.

In the Bible, the Holy Trinity is described as appearing to Abraham and his wife Sarah in the form of three angels. Icons of the Three Angels of the Trinity are to be found dating from the late 14th century onward, though few survive from this early period. The angels are normally depicted seated in repose, gesturing towards mystical symbols of divinity. They do not lend themselves to humanistic interpretation, but the three relaxed yet at the same time grave and tautly composed linear figures, combine to create some of the most compelling images in Russian iconography. The names of few icon painters from the 15th century are known to us, but, fortunately for Soviet art historians, the name of the painter of what is usually considered the most astonishingly beautiful 'Trinity' icon of all is known. It is Andrei Rublev. So instead of being forced to focus on the not-very-apparent humanity of the painting the historians are able to turn their attention to the artist. They emphasise his skill, they explain his technique, they place his work firmly in the emerging Russian national consciousness of the early 15th century. The artist is hero.

Questions 28–33

Do the statements below agree with the information in **Reading Passage 3**?
In Boxes 28–33, write:

Yes if the statement agrees with the information in the passage
No if the statement contradicts the information in the passage
Not Given if there is no information about the statement in the passage

> **Example:** The Soviet authorities are ambivalent towards the art of the Orthodox Church.
>
> **Answer:** Yes.

28. Icons have never been of much importance to Russian believers.

29. Soviet art historians have stressed the contribution of the Russian icon tradition to Russian cultural development in the 12th to 16th centuries.

30. To downplay the connection between Russian icons and Orthodox Christianity Russian icons were removed from churches and cathedrals and displayed in a secular setting.

31. The Tretyakov Art Gallery is home to paintings of a secular nature as well as religious paintings.

32. The spectator of the icons in the Tretyakov Art Gallery is invariably mesmerised by the sheer artistry of the works.

33. None of the works by Repin, Makovsky and Yaroshenko make fun of the religious beliefs of Russian peasants.

Questions 34–37

Choose the appropriate letters **A–D** and write them in Boxes 34–37 on your answer sheet.

34. The Tretyakov Art Gallery …

A only contains major religious paintings
B contains only icons
C contains a range of paintings from different eras
D is worth visiting according to the author

35. From the layout of the Tretyakov Art Gallery, spectators are meant to see …

A that Russian icons belong to a tradition which stresses the qualities of man and has nothing to do with God
B that Russian icons belong to a long religious tradition
C that Russian icons belong to a tradition which stresses the glory of God and diminishes the qualities of man
D that Russian icons belong to a tradition which celebrates the achievements of Russian peasants

36. Which of the following statements is true according to the passage?

A The icons in the Museum of Iconography come from different parts of Russia
B The Museum of Iconography contains only religious paintings from the 15th and 17th centuries
C The Museum of Iconography is the premier museum in the world for Russian icons
D The former Andonikov Monastery was destroyed to build the Museum of Iconography

37. The guidebooks for the Museum of Iconography …

A sing the praises of the original architects of the monastic complex
B point out the importance of the 15th century icons
C minimise the the religious significance of the monastery buildings
D stress the religious significance of the monastery buildings

Questions 38–40

Complete the sentences below. Use **NO MORE THAN THREE WORDS** from the passage for each blank space.

Write your answers in Boxes 38 – 40 on your answer sheet.

38. To secularising art historians, the Virgin was symbolic of __________.

39. The Three Angels of the Holy Trinity are not easily open to __________.

40. The artist of what is considered the most beautiful 'Trinity' icon in the world is celebrated by Soviet art historians as a __________.

Key

Key to Test 1

Questions 1 – 5

This type of question is a variation of paragraph headings. There are no distracters in this section, which makes it much easier.

1. **Answer: E**. The paragraph is about the fact that parameters help our minds to be creative.

2. **Answer: C**. The answer lies in the key phrases: ... *keeping creative ability in check* (in the first sentence) and *These limitations are needed so that once they are learnt, they can be broken* (the last sentence of the paragraph). The focus sentence is a combination of these two ideas. Note how the word *yet* divides the paragraph. It indicates the focus of the paragraph against the background in the first part. It also marks the division of information in the whole passage.

3. **Answer: A**. The writer wrote the paragraph to show that habits limit our creativity and the habits we need to survive play a role in this limitation.

4. **Answer: D**. The theme of the paragraph is how creativity works.

5. **Answer: B**. The paragraph deals with how parameters help the mind to be creative.

For further information re practice with information in paragraphs and with paragraph headings, see Exercises 1–12 and the Reading Tests in *A book for IELTS* by McCarter, Easton & Ash.

Questions 6 – 10

6. **Answer: C**. The answer is in the first line of the passage: *It is a myth that creative people are born with their talents*. Here, *it is a myth* = are not.

7. **Answer: C**. The answer is in paragraph A. The actual words are not in the paragraph, but the meaning is clear. **A** is not correct, because this is a myth; **B** is not correct, because the passage states that *when we try to be creative, our automatic response takes over*. **D** is not correct, because the *well-trodden paths* prevent creativity. Compare number 13 below.

8. **Answer: D**. The answer is in paragraph B: *Unfortunately, mankind's very struggle for survival has become a tyranny*. The answer paraphrases this statement. **A** is not correct, because the passage says the *struggle has become i.e.* ***is a tyranny***, not that it is becoming so; **B** is not correct, because cholesterol is not mentioned in relationship to the brain, but the mind. **C** is incorrect, because it is the mind which is circumscribed.

9. **Answer: A**. The answer is in paragraph C: *a continuous process of restrictions, which is increasing exponentially with the advancement of technology*. The statement is a paraphrase of this section. Note **B** and **C** are basically the same; it is, therefore, not possible to have either of these two alternatives as your answer. Watch out for this feature in multiple choice questions.

10. **Answer: D**. The answer is in paragraph C: *Is it surprising then that creative ability appears to be so rare*?. This is a question and has the same meaning as the statement given, i.e. it is not surprising. Note **C** is not possible, because the passage doesn't indicate whether the rarity is increasing or decreasing.

Questions 11 – 15

11. **Answer: Yes**. The answer is at the beginning of paragraph D: ... *and one that recognises that rules and regulations are parameters ....*

12. **Answer: Not Given**. There is no reference to this statement in the passage.

13. **Answer: Yes**. The answer is in paragraph D: *The difficulty in this exercise and with creation itself is convincing people that creation is possible*. The answer is a paraphrase of this part of the text. Compare number 7 above.

14. **Answer: Yes**. The answer is at the end of paragraph D: *leaving the safcty of one's own thought patterns is very much akin to madness;* akin to = like.

15. **Answer: Yes**. The answer is in the latter half of paragraph E.

Reading Passage 2

Questions 16–19

16. **Answer: B.** The answer is in the second sentence of paragraph 1: *we crave security.*

17. **Answer: B**. The answer is in paragraph 2. The key word is *increasingly* = becoming. **A**, **C** and **D** are all mentioned in the paragraph, but not in the correct context.

18. **Answer: A.** The answer is in the first sentence of paragraph 2: *now do not.* **B** is the opposite and **C** and **D** are just phrases lifted from the text.

19. **Answer: D**. The answer is in paragraph 3, the key phrase is *bar entry to the uninitiated*, which the answer paraphrases. **A** is incorrect, because only some access is not allowed. **B** is not true, because it is the working space that is compartmentalised, not the user, and **C** is not correct, because 'traps' are not the same as 'trappings'

Questions 20–27

Before you start looking in the text for the words to complete the blank spaces, you should read the summary through quickly to get an idea of the overall meaning. As you read, you should work out what kind of word you need to find in each case. For example, does the blank require a verb in the imperative form, a noun, an adjective or an adverb? You should also think of words that could fill the blanks so that when you look at the original passage the answers will come to you more easily.

20. **Answer: solved**. Although the word combat appears in the original, it does not fit here grammatically. The past participle is needed. Note *overcame* is the Simple Past, not the Past Participle.

21. **Answer: computers**. The plural is needed here.

22. **Answer: other people**.

23. **Answer: cut-off**. The word *isolating* does not fit grammatically. You need an adjective made from the past participle of the verb. Compare 20 above.

24. **Answer: team-work**.

25. **Answer: decrease in**.

26. **Answer: team-work**. As it says in the instructions, you may use a word or phrase more than once.

27. **Answer: just the same way as**. The answer is obviously not *similar* or *no different from*.

Questions 28–30

28. **Answer: touch-tone dialling systems**. The answer is in paragraph 7: *if we are unfortunate enough to contact an organization with a sophisticated touch-tone dialling system*. The key word here is *unfortunate*, which shows that the writer is negative about the topic. The writer does not comment on the other means of communication in the same way.

29. **Answer: electronic presence**. The answer is in paragraph 8.

30. **Answer: no longer geographical**. The answer is in paragraphs 8 and 9: *.. now that location is no longer geographical .... An example of this is the mobile phone*. The important thing here is to recognise the link between the paragraphs.

Reading Passage 3

Questions 31–36

31. **Answer: K**. The answer is in the first sentence of the passage. Note that the active needs to be changed into the passive.

32. **Answer: G**. The answer is in the first paragraph. B is not correct, because the passage says foods *may be* unique, not that they are and is not talking about ethnocentric properties.

33. **Answer: F**. The answer is in paragraph 3.

34. **Answer: J**. The answer is in paragraph 4. The key phrase is towards the end of the paragraph: *a cultural practice needs behavioural reinforcement*.

35 **Answer: E**. The answer is in the third paragraph.

36. **Answer: D**. The answer is in paragraph 6. C is incorrect, because it is the language and the cuisine that vary, not the link. And H is not correct. It is the character of language and cuisine that is said to be fundamental, and not language and cuisine themselves. Beware of the right word or phrase in the wrong context.

Questions 37–40

37. **Answer: B**. The answer is in paragraph 3. After scanning for the name, the important word is *distinction* which means difference in this case.

38. **Answer: D**. The answer is in the last paragraph.

39. **Answer: C**. The answer is in paragraph 2. The important thing here is to link correctly the names to the themes.

40. **Answer: A**. The answer is in paragraph 4.

Note how the answers in this section are jumbled; otherwise, it would be too easy!

Key to Test 2

Questions 1 – 8

1. **Answer: iv.** The paragraph is about the link between tea and hospitality. The answer is not iii, because the paragraph is about the continuing tradition of the past; it is not limited to Britain and China. It is tempting to put vii as the answer, but, if you look at the text, you will see that the information relating to this heading is between commas. It is additional information and can easily be removed. You can compare it to a non-defining relative clause. So it is not central to the meaning of the whole paragraph. Moreover, the passage states *in many parts of the world*, not *in all*. For more information on paragraph headings, see *A book for IELTS* by McCarter, Easton & Ash.

2. **Answer: viii**. The heading here should be fairly obvious.

3. **Answer: i**. The paragraph deals with the various ways in which tea has been drunk. The answer is not v; see paragraph H, where the whole paragraph deals with milk in relation to tea drinking. Compare the answer to Paragraph A for background/ foreground information.

4. **Answer: x**. The paragraph is about the cost of tea, in financial terms. The paragraph sets the scene, showing that tea is for the middle classes, but when the price falls the poor start drinking it. The answer is not xi, as value has a different meaning.

5. **Answer: ii**. The theme of the paragraph is the fact that most religious groups do not object to tea drinking, i.e. few do. The answer is not vi, as this does not reflect the theme of the paragraph. It is again subsidiary or background information. So it is important for you to see how the pieces of information in a paragraph relate to each other. A plan of the paragraph is as follows:

Foreground	**Background**
Few objections to tea drinking	
	In Islamic cultures no objection
	Tea/coffee versus alcohol
Seventh-Day Adventists/caffeine frowned upon	

Note how the points *in italics* give background information to the main point in the text. It is sometimes difficult for students to make the distinction between these two types of information. The example of the Islamic cultures supports the point of there being no objections. The second piece of background information develops this further comparing tea/coffee with alcohol. The paragraph then comes back to the central issue of there being few objections, by giving the example of a group who object to tea. Use this mechanism to look at the other paragraphs here and elsewhere.

6. **Answer: xii**. This paragraph focuses on tea drinking in Africa. The answer is not ix, as the origin of the tea itself is not said to be African.

7. **Answer: v**. The paragraph is about the importance of the addition of milk to tea in many parts of the world. Compare paragraph C. Heading xii would not be right here, as it describes only part of the paragraph.

8. **Answer: iii**. See the answer for paragraph A.

Questions 9 – 14

9. **Answer: rituals of hospitality/hospitality**. The answer is in paragraph A. The first phrase is probably the better of the two.

10. **Answer: grade(s) and blend(s)/different grades/different blends**. The answer is in the last sentence of paragraph D.

11. **Answer: contains caffeine**. The answer is in paragraph E. Because of the word limit and the grammar of the sentence in the exercise, the words *the stimulant* cannot be included.

12. **Answer: nomadic Bedouin/Bedouin/Bedouins/nomadic Bedouins**. The answer is in paragraph F.

13. **Answer: sugar and spices**. The answer is in paragraph H. Because of the word limit, the word *some* has to be excluded from the phrase.

14. **Answer: lingering convention/convention**. The answer is in the second sentence in last paragraph.

Reading Passage 2

Questions 15 – 18

15. **Answer: A**. The answer is in paragraph 1. A tye is not large, so **B** is not correct. We do not know if there were trees, so **C** is not correct. And **D** was not always the case.

16. **Answer: C**. The answer is in the first sentence of the second paragraph. The answer is not **A** or **B**, because the text does not indicate any degree of possibility/probability, nor does it state a specific number. **D** is obviously wrong.

17. **Answer: C**. The answer is in paragraph 2, in the first sentence: *... all except one at the margins of the parish.* **A** is not correct– see the second sentence of the paragraph. **B** is 'likely', but the answer is not categorically given. **D** is incorrect, because *most*, not all, of the land was owned by the Priory.

18. **Answer: D**. The answer is in paragraph 2. Note the tense: *... would, in any case, have been unattractive...*, indicating what the writer interprets as having happened. Note that the word *unattractive* here does not mean visually. It means that they would not have liked it, because it was not producing anything. So **A** and **B** are wrong because they talk about *sight*. **C** is obviously wrong.

Questions 19 – 29

In this section you just have to follow the dates. However, you still need to be careful. The answers in this section span paragraphs 3 – 6.

19. **Answer: documented**. This is in the first sentence of paragraph 3. It means the name is found in books or documents of the time.

20. **Answer: in use**. This is in the second sentence of paragraph 3.

21. **Answer: cropping up/and crops up/and cropped up**. The answer is in the second sentence of paragraph 3. Note the different tenses and the verb forms here. You can change the present simple *crops up* into the gerund and you can use the simple past tense. They all fit the grammar of the text in the exercise.

22. **Answer: File's Green**. The answer is in the third sentence of paragraph 3.

23. **Answer: burnt down/abandoned**. The answers are at end of paragraph 3. Both answers are correct.

24. **Answer: owned.** The answer is in the first sentence of paragraph 4. You need to change the word *ownership* to a verb to fit the grammar here.

25. **Answer: two/two brick**. The answer is in the first sentence of paragraph 4.

26. **Answer: each one/each/each cottage**. The answer is in paragraph 4. The last phrase is possible, but it does involve repetition of the word *cottage*.

27. **Answer: remained/survived**. The first answer is in the last sentence of the penultimate paragraph. The latter word occurs elsewhere in the text.

28. **Answer: gravel works**. The answer is in the last paragraph. Note this phrase is an adjective here. Note that you cannot add the word *newly-opened*. In the reading passage the word describes the word *works*, but in the exercise it would describe the word *manager*!

29. **Answer: one dwelling**. The answer is in the last paragraph. Note that there were two cottages. Each cottage had two families, i.e. two dwellings. One cottage was destroyed leaving one cottage with two dwellings, which the manager converted into a cottage with one dwelling. Note you cannot have the word *one* on its own.

Reading Passage 3

Questions 30–32

30. **Answer: B**. The answer is in paragraph 1. The passage states that Haydn composed the London symphony *for* London, but not where he composed it.

31. **Answer: B**. The answer is in the first paragraph. **A** is incorrect, because some were written in the following century. **C** is not right, because the last sentence of the paragraph says the opposite, and **D** is incorrect, because only the oratorios and masses were full of religious feeling.

32. **Answer: D**. The answer is in paragraph 3, the first sentence and later in paragraph 5 where he talks about Opus 77. **A** is incorrect, because they were the result not the cause of a spiritual crisis. **B** is incorrect, because this phrase describes a *musical form* and is not complete – in paragraph 2. **C** is not right, because it doesn't make sense.

Questions 33–37

33. **Answer: tense** (not long-breathed). See sentence 2 of paragraph 3 for the comparison.

34. **Answer: Unlike** (not like). See the comparison in paragraph 3, the key phrase being *far from*.

35. **Answer: more** (not less). See paragraph 4.

36. **Answer: quieter** (not subdued). As in 35, be wary of paraphrased comparisons.

37. **Answer: Conversely** (not similarly). see paragraph 4.

Questions 38–40

38. **Answer: No**. The answer is in the second sentence of paragraph 5, the key phrase being *almost immediately*, i.e. after.

39. **Answer: Yes**. The answer is in the first sentence of the last paragraph.

40. **Answer: Yes**. The whole passage gives the reader this impression. See, for example, the end of the first paragraph and the last sentence of the passage.

Key to Test 3

Questions 1–5

1. **Answer: D**. The answer is in the first paragraph. The key word is *erroneously*. B is incorrect, as it is the opposite of what the passage says.

2. **Answer: H.** The answer is in the second paragraph, in the first part of the second sentence: *Human nature has an inclination for pessimism and anxiety*. Notice how the second sentence here explains why doom-mongers will never be out of business. And notice how you anticipate that an explanation is needed as you read the first sentence. This type of question is testing your ability to understand the relationship between information across sentences.

3. **Answer: I**. The answer is in paragraph 2 where catastrophes in the past and present are compared: ... *is that the catastrophes are more 'in your face'*, i.e. immediate.

4. **Answer: K**. The answer is in the latter half of the second paragraph.

5. **Answer: J**. The answer is in paragraph 3. The sentence is in effect a summary of the paragraph. Note how the writer interchanges government, politicians and ministers in the paragraph.

Questions 6–9

6. **Answer: D**. The answer can be found in the first sentence of the fifth paragraph. Note that *delude* means *deceive*; look at the title for this section in the passage. **A** is not true, because it is the opposite of the correct answer. **B** is not mentioned and **C** is not possible, because in the last sentence of the paragraph, it says *people are manipulated by their fears*.

7. **Answer: C**. The answer is in paragraph 5. **A** is not correct, because it doesn't say whether market research uses people's fears to help them; it says that it takes advantage of them, i.e. manipulates/exploits them. **B** and **D** are not correct, because the text does not mention any information about either.

8. **Answer: C**. The answer is in paragraph 7: *they are the driving force behind success*. The word *they* refers to the feelings mentioned previously. **A** is incorrect, because the passage talks about 'if' not 'when': ... *if properly harnessed* .... **B** is incorrect, because it is feelings that are said to be the driving force behind success (not the engines of genius). **D** is wrong, because the writer says it is the feelings listed which are usually associated with failure.

9. **Answer: B**. The answer is in the eighth paragraph. **A** and **D** are obviously wrong and **C** is the opposite.

Questions 10 – 14

10. **Answer: Not Given**. The text does not say anything about this.

11. **Answer: Yes**. The answer is in paragraph 8.

12. **Answer: Yes**. The answer is in the first sentence of the penultimate paragraph.

13. **Answer: Not Given**. The answer is in the penultimate paragraph. The text does not tell us what the writer believes about Nostradamus's predictions or those of the other prophets either.

14. **Answer: No**. The answer is in the last sentence. The word *sanguine* means *hopeful*.

Questions 15–22

15. **Answer: glamour**. The answer is in the first sentence of the second paragraph.

16. **Answer: research**. The answer is in the second paragraph towards the end.

17. **Answer: editing process**. The answer is in paragraph 3, the fourth sentence. The phrase *first draft* does not fit here, as the sentence would not then reflect the meaning of the passage. Nor is the word *writing* correct for the same reason. And it would not fit the grammar of the summary; the article *the* in the summary would have to be omitted, as the writer is talking about all writers writing not specifically himself.

18. **Answer: summary**. The answer is at the end of the fourth paragraph. Note the word *summary* is a synonym for *synopsis/ outline*.

19. **Answer: readers**. At the start of the sixth paragraph it says that *readers* (not publishers) *vet books*.

20. **Answer: Alterations**. The answer is in the sixth paragraph.

21. **Answer: writing**. The answer is in the last paragraph. The word *publishing* is not correct, because the writer is talking about writing throughout the passage; publishing comes afterwards.

22. **Answer: ups and downs**. The answer is in the last paragraph. Note the word *roller-coaster* is not possible here. It does not make sense. The word does not carry the meaning of the latter part of the last sentence on its own. Nor is it grammatically possible: the summary has a plural verb and the word *roller-coaster* is singular.

Questions 23 and 24

23. **Answer: A**. The answer is a paraphrase of the last sentence of paragraph 2*: Sometimes, instinct takes the place of market research ....* **B** is the opposite. As for **C,** the text does not say whether it is essential. **D** is not correct, because the text says *sometimes*–therefore, note the word *can* in **A**.

24. **Answer: D**. The answer is a paraphrase of the penultimate sentence of the third paragraph. **A** is not correct, because although the text says that *a passage may end up nothing remotely like the* original, the writer does not say that this is a problem. **B** is not possible, because the writer does not say the use is unfortunate; he is expressing an opinion, when he says *unfortunately*. **C** is incorrect, because the problem is not a luxury.

Questions 25–28

25. **Answer: appraisal**. The answer is at the beginning of paragraph 4.

26. **Answer: some invaluable advice/invaluable advice/some advice/advice/hints**. The answer is in the fifth paragraph. Note you cannot give the examples here as there would be too many words. You can use the word *hints* from the last sentence of the paragraph as it is a synonym, which summarises the advice and the examples.

27. **Answer: radical redrafting/redrafting/reworkings/text amputations**. The answer is at the end of paragraph 6.

28. **Answer: creation period**. The answer is in the last sentence of paragraph 6.

Questions 29–35

29. **Answer: iii**. The predictions made did not happen, i.e. *...failed to materialise*. The answer is not heading viii, as the text does not say that working hours have been reduced to 25 hours–it was an estimate of 25 to 30 hours.

30. **Answer: i**. The first sentence is the topic sentence and the rest of the paragraph expands the theme. Note heading iv is not the answer. The focus of the paragraph is on the increase in leisure spending. The writer compares it briefly to other areas, i.e. food, housing and transport, but this is not part of the main focus of the paragraph. In any case, the heading would have to include housing and transport as well as food. Note that this paragraph contains general information about leisure in relation to the more specific comparison in the next two paragraphs. Note also the word *strongly* in heading i.

31 **Answer: iv**. The paragraph explains that spending on food has decreased, while that for leisure has increased. Heading x is not the correct answer as this is too general. Nor is heading i possible. See the explanation for 30 above. Some students may be tempted to put heading v as the answer, but this relates only to the first part of the paragraph and does not cover the contrast between leisure and food.

The correct heading here is the same as that for the next paragraph, i.e. the example. Read the instructions at the beginning of the exercise.

32. **Answer: xiii**. The paragraph talks about all three going up and gives an example of leisure in the future. Heading vi is not correct as this relates only to part of the paragraph.

33. **Answer: xi**. Heading ix is not the answer as the text does not say whether the 'grey pound' is becoming stronger or not.

34. **Answer: vii**. The first sentence is the topic sentence. The answer is not iii as the paragraph does not say that the forecasts are false.

35. **Answer: xiv**. The paragraph deals with the two aspects, wealth and leisure hours.

Questions 36 – 40

36. **Answer: No**. The answer is in paragraph A. The predicted reduction in working hours did not happen.

37. **Answer: Yes**. The answer is in the first sentence of paragraph B.

38. **Answer: No**. The answer is in the middle of paragraph E; the opposite is true.

39. **Answer: Not Given**. It does not mention this anywhere in the passage. You just have to look at the sections of the text relating to the future, i.e. the end of paragraph E and all of G.

40. **Answer: Not Given**. The answer is in paragraph G. The writer does not say whether the 24-hour society will affect people's attitudes.

KEY to Test 4

Questions 1 – 3

1. **Answer: vi**. The answer is in paragraph 3. The answer is not v, because there is no mention of when the HMI was created.

2. **Answer: iii**. The answer is in the fourth paragraph. Note that vii is not possible, because the passage says the report was *seminal*, i.e. important/influential.

3. **Answer: i**. The answer is in paragraph 4.

Questions 4 – 8

4. **Answer: endangering their job**. The answer is in the first paragraph. The sentence is a paraphrase of the first sentence of the text.

5. **Answer: [mainly] liberal**. The answer is at the beginning of the last sentence of the first paragraph.

6. **Answer: widen/widening participation**. The answer is in the second paragraph. Note that the gerund can be changed to the infinitive.

7. **Answer: academic staff's explanations**. The answer is in the second sentence of the third paragraph.

8. **Answer: reduction of taxes/tax reduction**. The answer is in the first sentence of the fourth paragraph. The verb phrase in the passage needs to be changed into a noun phrase to fit the sentence given.

Questions 9 – 14

9. **Answer: C**. The answer is in the fourth paragraph. **A** is incorrect, as this was not what the report did. **B** is not right, as the report did not give the money, and **D** is incomplete.

10. **Answer: C**. The answer is in paragraph 4. **A** is not right, because the money is not given to the student (it is given to the college for the student). **B** is incorrect, because it was the further education that became quasi-independent, not the principles, and **D** is not possible, as the text does not say this.

11. **Answer: A**. The answer can be found in the first sentence of the fifth paragraph. The phrase *to reduce the student drop-out rate* is a paraphrase of *to improve retention*. It is important to look out for ways in which sections of the text are paraphrased in the various types of questions. **B, C** and **D** are incorrect, because all three contain phrases lifted from the text, but used here in the wrong context.

12. **Answer: A**. The answer can be found in the second sentence of the fifth paragraph. Note that the sentence gives three complexities, which hinder the reducing of drop-out rates. **B** is not mentioned in the text, nor is **C**. The first element of **D** is correct, but the second one is nonsensical.

13. **Answer: D**. The answer is in the second half of the fifth paragraph. The last sentence gives the answer, i.e: something other than data. **A** and **B** are not stated, and **C** is incomplete.

14. **Answer: B**. The answer is in the final paragraph, and is a summary of the examples given. **A** is a phrase lifted from the text and is part of two ideas – note the comma in the text. **C** is incorrect, because the passage refers to raising the students' expectations, not those of the college. **D** is not correct, because Martinez outlined the strategies, so Martinez's summary included the strategies, and not the other way round.

Reading Passage 2

Questions 15 – 19

15. **Answer: C**. The answer is in the first paragraph. G is incorrect, because it is the opposite of what the text says.

16. **Answer: I**. The answer is in paragraph 2, in the second sentence. B is incorrect, because it is not mentioned as an aspect of management of one's emotions, but as a means of managing them.

17. **Answer: E**. The answer can be found in the second part of paragraph 2, and is a paraphrase of the sixth sentence. A is incorrect, as it is our emotions that are said to empower and hinder us.

18. **Answer: H**. The answer is at the start of the third paragraph.

19. **Answer: F**. The answer is in the fourth sentence of paragraph 3. D is incorrect, because it is emotions that are said to be not tangible, not handling relationships. It is important to be very wary of words or phrases that are lifted directly from the text. They are often put into the wrong context.

Questions 20 – 26

20. **Answer: C**. The answer is in the first paragraph, in the latter half of the first sentence. Alternative D is not possible, because it says *at least 5*, while the text says *5*.

21. **Answer: C**. The answer can be found in paragraph 2. **A** is not possible, as the text advises against suppressing or hindering emotions. The same applies to **B**. **D** does not make sense.

22. **Answer: C**. The answer is in the fifth sentence of the third paragraph. **A** is incorrect, because the text does not say this, and it is incomplete. **B** is incorrect, because the text says *quantify* and the exercise *qualify*. **D** is not the right answer, because it is not complete and is nonsense.

23. **Answer: D**. The answer is in the third paragraph, in the second sentence from the end. **A** is not stated. **B** is incorrect, because the text says ... *can cost money* ... i.e. not always. **C** is a phrase from the text, but is not used in the right context here.

24. **Answer: B**. The answer can be found in the last sentence of the third paragraph. Alternative **A** is not mentioned in the text and the words included in **C** appear in the text, but do not fit here. **D** is grammatically incorrect.

25. **Answer: A**. The answer is in the second sentence of the penultimate paragraph. The other alternatives are obviously wrong.

26. **Answer:** C. The answer is in the last paragraph, in the last sentence, *becoming less frequent* is a paraphrase of *fast disappearing*. **A** is untrue, because the text does not say this. **B** is incorrect, because it is people who need to be re-skilled, and **D** does not make sense.

Question 27

27. **Answer: Not Given**. The answer can be found in the last paragraph. The author says it is sad that people need to be re-skilled, but does not mention whether the lack of Emotional Intelligence will lead to anything.

Reading Passage 3

Questions 28 – 30

28. **Answer: vi**. The answer is in the third paragraph in the first sentence. i is incorrect, because it was an anthropologist friend of Koestler who said this. ii is not correct, because Koestler was talking about his friends rather than immigrants in general; and v is not stated as a general principle.

29. **Answer: ii**. The answer is in paragraph 3, in the last sentence. vi is incorrect, because Fishberg was talking about immigrants in general, not his friends.

30. **Answer: iv**. The answer can be found in the fourth paragraph, in the second sentence. iii is incorrect, because Emerson says this is a mistaken impression.

Questions 31 – 36

31. **Answer: Not Given**. The text does not mention anything about this statement.

32. **Answer: No**. The answer can be found in paragraph 4, in the last sentence: *a completely different and no less important issue*, which means, in effect, equally important.

33. **Answer: Yes**. The answer is in the second sentence of paragraph 5. The word *these* refers back to *speech organs*.

34. **Answer: Not Given**. The answer is in the same place as question 33. The passage says that practice is needed to learn new phonemes, but does not mention whether or not they are difficult to learn.

35. **Answer: Yes**. The answer is at the end of paragraph 5. The words *parody* and *mock* are synonyms of *make fun of*.

36. **Answer: Not Given**. The text does not mention anything about this statement.

Questions 37 – 40

37. **Answer: D**. The answer is in paragraph 7, and is a paraphrase *of help their students acquire the distinctive sound of the target pronunciation*. F is incorrect, as it is incomplete.

38. **Answer: A**. This answer can also be found in the seventh paragraph. A mental aid is said to be *employed* i.e. *used*. I is incorrect, because the cause and effect are the wrong way round. H is not correct, because there is no mention of which of the two accents is easier.

39. **Answer: E**. The answer is in the first part of the last paragraph. B is incorrect, because it is the answer to the question that is said to be irrelevant.

40. **Answer: G**. The answer is in the second part of the last paragraph. C is incorrect, because it is not pronunciation that is worth investigating, but the link between pronunciation and physiognomy.

Key to Test 5

Reading Passage 1

Questions 1 – 5

1. **Answer: D**. The answer is in the first paragraph. The author does not say what he believes. **A** and **B** are incorrect, because the writer says: ...*we hear about*.... ; not that he believes it one way or the other. Nor does the text state whether he is sure or not as in **C**. Also, look at the last paragraph.

2. **Answer: C**. The answer is in the last sentence of the first paragraph. The key phrase is *as is so often the case*. Therefore, **A** and **B** are not possible. As for **D**, the text does not tell you this.

3. **Answer: D**. The answer is in the second paragraph, in the last sentence. **A** does not relate to what the meteorologists believe. See earlier in the paragraph. **B** is not correct, because it is the opposite. **C** is incorrect, because the meteorologists do not say that the results will be devastating.

4. **Answer: D**. The answer is in the first part of paragraph 3, in the first sentence. **A** is the opposite of the correct answer. **B** and **C** appear in the text, but in a different context.

5. **Answer: A**. The answer is in the second part of paragraph 3: *using artificial models of climate as a way of predicting change is all but impossible*. **B** is incorrect, because this is what Dr Hansen said in the past; the same is true for **C**. **D** is incorrect, because Dr Hansen does not say anything about Earth getting colder, only greener.

Questions 6 – 11

6. **Answer: Not Given**. The answer can be found in paragraph 4. The text does not say anything about the weather forecaster's expertise.

7. **Answer: No**. The answer is in the second part of the fourth paragraph. The opposite is true, as most of the increase happened before the second half of the twentieth century.

8. **Answer: Yes**. The answer can be found in the first sentence of the fifth paragraph. Also see paragraph 1.

9. **Answer: Not Given**. This is not mentioned in the passage. Look in paragraph 5.

10. **Answer: Not Given**. This is not mentioned in the passage. Look in paragraph 6.

11. **Answer: Yes**. The answer can be found in the second part of the last paragraph.

Questions 12 and 13

12. **Answer: in recycled paper**. The answer is in the last paragraph. The elements of the sentence have been changed around.

13. **Answer: most to lose**. The answer can be found in the last paragraph. Again the elements of sentence have been changed around.

Question 14

14. **Answer: B**. The writer wrote the passage to show that the issue of global warming is often exaggerated by the press. The other titles refer to only parts of the text. You would be wise to leave this question until you have answered all the other questions, so that you have a better feel for the text.

Reading Passage 2

Questions 15 – 21

15. **Answer: vi**. The paragraph is about the fact that there are two distinct superorders in the classification of Reptilia. Note heading iii is incorrect; the idea being that they are not *terrible lizards*. Look at the word *although* at the start of the paragraph.

16. **Answer: xi**. The paragraph talks about the origins of both lepidosaurs and archosaurs, in the Triassic period. Heading ix is therefore incorrect, as this covers only part of the content of the paragraph.

17. **Answer: xiii**. Heading i is incorrect, as this is a reference only to a detail in the paragraph.

18. **Answer: vii**. The second sentence of the paragraph is the topic sentence, which gives the theme of the paragraph. You also need to look at the end of the paragraph for the word *unique*. Heading ii is incorrect, as the paragraph is talking about features which distinguish dinosaurs from other animals and other archosaurs.

19. **Answer: iv**. The answer is in the first two sentences of the paragraph, which the rest of the paragraph expands upon. Heading xii is incorrect, as this heading covers only part of the paragraph.

20. **Answer: v**. The paragraph deals with the suborders of Saurischia.

21. **Answer: viii**. The answer is in the first sentence of the paragraph.

Questions 22 – 24

22. **Answer: skeletal anatomy**. The answer is in paragraph A. Note how the information is presented in a different order in the paragraph. Note how the text as a whole hangs around this key phrase.

23. **Answer: eosuchians**. The answer is in the last sentence of paragraph B. Note, again, how the order of the information has been changed, but the meaning of the sentence is the same.

24. **Answer: two long bones.** The answer is in the second half of paragraph C. The use of the colon is important here. The answer therefore needs to be an explanation of the word *vomers*. It is important to check the word limit, not all of the information about vomers in the passage can be included here.

Questions 25 – 28

25. **Answer: B**. The answer is at the end of paragraph D. E is incorrect as this refers to lizards, and not to dinosaurs. See the middle of paragraph D.

26. **Answer: G**. The answer is in the third sentence of paragraph E: *All dinosaurs had a pelvic girdle with each side comprised of three bones*. (i.e six bones). The answer is not A, because in the first sentence it says that dinosaurs are divided into two orders, and in paragraph F that Saurischia was divided into two suborders, but, in paragraph G, Ornithischia into three suborders.

27. **Answer: H**. The answer can be found in paragraph F. It is important to note the word *unlike* in the first part of the sentence. C is incorrect, because both could be heavy.

28. **Answer: F**. The answer is in paragraph G. The first part of the sentence refers to the ornithopods, the second part to the thyreophorans. D is incorrect, because this phrase refers to the dinosaurs mentioned in the first part of the sentence, not the second.

Reading Passage 3

Questions 29 – 32

29. **Answer: Yes**. The answer is in the last sentence of paragraph 2.

30. **Answer: Not Given**.

31. **Answer: Yes**. The answer is at the beginning of paragraph 3; 1690 is in the 17th century.

32. **Answer: No**. The answer is in the first sentence of paragraph 4; it is not strange but *understandable* that people are sceptical.

Questions 33 – 36

33. **Answer: D**. The answer is in paragraph 4, in the second sentence. **A** is incorrect because *combining the senses in a public display* in the passage, does not have the same meaning as **A**. **B** is incorrect, as the passage does not mention frequency. **C** is incorrect, because the word *involuntary* does not have the same meaning as in the passage.

34. **Answer: C**. The answer is to be found in paragraph 5, in both the second and the third sentences. **A** is incorrect, because the passage states that they did have these abilities. **B** is incorrect as the meaning of *well-documented* is *recorded in detail*. And **D** is incorrect, because there is no mention of any agreement in the text.

35. **Answer: C**. Paragraph 6 talks about Wassily Kandinsky, and the answer is in the last sentence. **A** is incorrect, as he was *at a performance*, not in one. **B** is not right, because *found* does not have the same meaning as *founded*. **D** is incorrect, because it is not complete.

36. **Answer: A**. The answer is in paragraph 7, in the second sentence. **B** is incorrect, because it is the knowledge that is a revelation, not the people. **C** is not right, because no mention is made of inferiority or superiority. And **D** is not right, because there is no mention of this.

Questions 37 – 40

37 – 40. **Answers: A, C, E, F**. The answers can be found in paragraphs 7. A and F are in the fifth sentence of paragraph 7. E in the fourth sentence of the same paragraph. C is at the end of the paragraph. The distracters are wrong for the following reasons: B is incorrect, because in paragraph 7 it says: *It is not unusual for people who have synaesthesia to be creative.....*'. D is incorrect, because it is the condition not the people that have the drawbacks. (see the first sentence of paragraph 8). And G is not correct, because as the last sentence of paragraph 8 says, the link between colour and writing is not meant literally.

Key to Test 6

Reading Passage 1

Questions 1–10

Remember to read the summary through quickly to get an idea of the overall meaning in the text. Then complete the blank spaces. Look at the Key for the second Reading Passage in Test 1.

1. **Answer: Imagine**.

2. **Answer: citizen**.

3. **Answer: crocodile**.

4. **Answer: obelisk**.

5. **Answer: obelisk**. Remember that the instructions said that you could use a word more than once and this is it. Note that the word *features* is a verb. Therefore, a noun as a subject is required here.

6. **Answer: Pharaoh**.

7. **Answer: uprising**.

8. **Answer: mind/minds**.

9. **Answer: propaganda**.

10. **Answer: subtle**. If you read the gap-filling exercise, without looking at the passage, you may come up with the adjective *good*, but the word *good* is not in the passage. Still this should help you to find the answer, as you read the text.

Questions 11 – 14

11. **Answer: D**. The answer is in paragraph 5: *propaganda is simply a process of* ***persuasion***.

12. **Answer: D**. The answer is in paragraph 5, in the last sentence. You have to be careful here as the inclination for most people is to put **C** as the answer. However, the writer is talking about the time before 1914. Compare the use of the present simple when you describe the graph in Task 1 of the writing Test: T*he graph shows..., From 1950 to 1960 sales rise....* In the latter case the present simple is used to describe the past! You could in the latter case use the simple past. Also look at newspaper headlines. Note also the first sentence of the next paragraph: *It is unlikely ... that propaganda will ever be rehabilitated as a neutral concept* (i.e. as it was before 1914).

13. **Answer: A**. The answer is in paragraph 7. Note that **B** and **C** are the opposite of the answer and **D** is obviously nonsense.

14. **Answer: B**. The answer is in the last sentence of the last paragraph. The expression *to be had* means to be deceived. Note that the public knows the deception is happening and agrees to it*: but we don't know if they are happy about it.*

Reading Passage 2

Questions 15 – 21

15. **Answer: English lexicographer**. The answer is in the first line of paragraph 1. Note you cannot put the word *great* because of the word *an*. Nor can you use the word *lexicographer* on its own for the same reason.

16. **Answer: (of) human knowledge**. The answer is in the first sentence of paragraph 2.

17. **Answer: advent of printing**. The answer is towards the end of paragraph 2. Note you cannot use the word *momentous*, because of the phrase *all important*. Some may be tempted to write *first revolution* which is found in the last sentence of the paragraph. The advent of printing is the first revolution in information technology, but if you use the phrase *first revolution*, the sense of the sentence is not complete.

18. **Answer: Renaissance man**. The answer is in the second sentence of paragraph 4.

19. **Answer: easy access to information/easily accessible information/easy information access**. The answer is in the penultimate sentence of paragraph 4.

20. **Answer: all-knowing**. The answer is in the last sentence of paragraph 4.

21. **Answer: stream of information**. The answer is in the first sentence of paragraph 5.

Note that in this section you are scanning the text for specific information. Note that sometimes the sentences for completion in the exercise may contain synonyms of words in the reading passage. Or the sentence for completion may be a paraphrase of the text. Be prepared to scan for *meaning, and not just words*.

Questions 22–25

22. **Answer: the most singular failure**. The answer is in the last sentence of paragraph 5.

23. **Answer: a natural human instinct**. The answer is in the first sentence of paragraph 6. Note the paraphrase here in the question.

24. **Answer: a vortex/a veritable vortex/a large information machine**. The answer is in the middle of paragraph 6. Note the word limit means you have to change the word order for the second alternative.

25. **Answer: disillusionment and stress**. The answer is in the last sentence of paragraph 6.

Questions 26 – 28

26. **Answer: No**. The answer is in the first sentence of paragraph 7.

27. **Answer: Not Given**.

28. **Answer: No**. The answer is in paragraph 9. The phrase *not all it is cracked up to be* means *not as good or beneficial as people believe*.

Reading Passage 3

Questions 29–33

29. **Answer: C.**

30. **Answer: E.**

31. **Answer: B.**

32. **Answer: D.**

33. **Answer: A.**

Questions 34–37

34. **Answer: Not Given**. The answer is in paragraph 5. Scan the text for the name and the date. We have only information about people living in the castle before 1639. The text mentions the castle fell into a state of disrepair, but nothing about people living there. Note the double negative in the statement.

35. **Answer: Yes**. The answer is in the last sentence of paragraph 5: *... it is redolent of another age, another dream.*

36. **Answer: Yes**. The answer is in the first sentence of paragraph 6: ... *1500-odd men* means more than 1500.

37. **Answer: Yes**. The answer is in the first sentence of paragraph 7: *Someone once said ... But it is certainly well worth a visit.*

Questions 38–40

38. **Answer: A**. The answer is in the latter half of paragraph 7. It is a summary of the feelings described in this part of the text. **B** and **D** are basically the same and so neither of them can be the answer! Alternative **C** is obviously wrong.

39. **Answer: B.**

40. **Answer: D**. Alternatives **A** and **B** reflect only part of the text. As for **C**, the direction of the *journey* is West to East!

Key to Test 7

Reading Passage 1

Questions 1 – 8

Note that each passage in this practice test has a section on headings. Some candidates make the mistake of reacting emotionally to this type of question. If they see it in the first reading passage, they then go to the next one and do the first passage last. This is not wise. The questions relating to the passages become more difficult. So candidates reduce their chances of obtaining a high score. It is, therefore, better to approach the passages logically; and to train oneself to do so. In this test, you cannot jump to the end as *each passage has headings*.

1. **Answer: viii**. The answer is not heading xii. The text does not say whether Lotte was a postgraduate student or not. Also being a student relates only to part of the information in the paragraph.
2. **Answer: v**. Some people may be tempted to choose xiii as the answer. This heading is not possible, as the paragraph is talking about a change in interest from socio-linguistics to texts and the book. So it is the opposite of the answer which is required.
3. **Answer: x**. Heading i is not possible, because it refers only to part of the information in the paragraph. It is part of the development of Wytze's work and is part of the subsidiary information which gives you the correct heading.
4. **Answer: vi**. Heading vii is incorrect, because there is no indication as to whether the work mentioned is to be published or not.
5. **Answer: ii**.
6. **Answer: ix**.
7. **Answer: xiv**. Again, the distracter iv is not possible, because Wytze's research was not restricted to Oxford. Nor does the paragraph just talk about research.
8. **Answer: xi**. Heading xv relates only to one piece of information in the first sentence. Be careful with reading only first and last sentences of paragraphs to work out a paragraph heading.

The passage is long, but the headings are fairly straightforward.

Questions 9 – 14

9. **Answer: Yes**. The answer is in paragraph A.
10. **Answer: Yes**. The answer is in paragraph B. Note the phrase *prior to*, which means before.
11. **Answer: No**. The answer is in paragraph C; in the latter half of the first sentence. Note how the word *should* indicates Wytze's opinion, not the writer's.
12. **Answer: Not Given**. Look at the information in paragraphs E and F.
13. **Answer: Yes**. The answer is in paragraph H. Note that Lotte worked in Amsterdam only during part of the 60s and 70s.
14. **Answer: No**. The answer is in paragraph I.

Question 15

15. **Answer: A**. The answer here is fairly obvious.

Reading Passage 2

Questions 16 – 20

16. **Answer: i**. Heading x is not a suitable answer. It has just been lifted from the introductory sentence of the paragraph. Be careful with relying on reading just the first and the last sentences of paragraphs.

17. **Answer: vi**.

18. **Answer: iv**. Heading ii does not work, as it relates only to one piece of information in the paragraph.

19. **Answer: viii**. Heading vii is not correct, because it again relates to one detail in the paragraph.

20. **Answer: ix**. Heading v relates only to a detail in the paragraph.

Questions 21 – 27

21 **Answer: Yes**. The answer is in the latter half of paragraph A.

22. **Answer: Yes**. The answer is in paragraph B and the rest of the passage after that. Note how the statement in the exercise is very wide, i.e. general. It covers/paraphrases the meaning in the paragraph: *... something momentous had occurred ..... to wipe out party ideology*, i.e. it affected it.

23. **Answer: Yes**. The answer is in the first sentence of paragraph C.

24. **Answer: Not Given**. The answer is in paragraph E. The text does not say anything about the Independent Whigs having large country estates. We can work out that most owned land, *invariably country gentlemen*, but we know nothing about the estates themselves. Note incidentally that the exercise says all as opposed to *invariably country gentlemen*, i.e. most. However, we are looking at the whole statement not part of it, so the answer cannot be No.

25. **Answer: Yes**. The answer is at the end of paragraph E.

26. **Answer: No**. The answer is in paragraph F.

27. **Answer: Not Given**. See the end of paragraph F. We do not know if Harris's analysis was used by Namier to support his views. We only know the results of Harris's analysis.

Reading Passage 3

Questions 28–35

28. **Answer: xii.**

29. **Answer: iii.**

30. **Answer: vi.**

31. **Answer: viii.**

32. **Answer: ix.**

33. **Answer: i.**

34. **Answer: xi.**

35. **Answer: iv**. Note that xiii is not the answer. The paragraph is not about *a swinging pendulum*. The pendulum has swung from one side to the other.

Questions 36–40

36. **Answer: D**. The answer is in paragraph A. **A** is not suitable, because the text talks about the change in attitude being brought about by *the demystification of medicine*. **B** is not suitable, because the text does not say whether the attitude change has led to a considerable improvement. And **C** is nonsense.

37. **Answer: A**. The answer is in paragraph F. **B** is not suitable, because it is the opposite of what is in the text. **C** is not suitable, because it is the opposite; compare **B**. As for **D**, the text is not about all medical personnel, but about doctors.

38. **Answer: D**. Alternative **A** is not suitable, because the writer indicates throughout that the text that he is for the changes; nowhere does it indicate that he has not made up his mind about them. **B** is not suitable, because it contradicts the writer's views and **C** is not suitable because, from the tone of the passage, it is clear that he supports the measures.

39. **Answer: A**. Alternative **B** is not suitable, because this heading relates to only part of the idea in the text. The heading in alternative **C** does not relate to the text. The passage is about the shift to a more patient-oriented service rather than a general look at medical training. As regards **D**, the text does not indicate this at all. Note a *panacea* is a *cure-all.*

40. **Answer: B**. **A** is not suitable, because the writer is definitely not criticising the change in attitude. Note that the text is primarily about the shift in public attitude, and not about developments in medicine (See 39**A**). **C** is not suitable, as the text does not talk about the need for changes, but a change that has taken place. Alternative **D** does not relate to the text.

    Note how the answer here relates to the answer for 39 above. The purpose helps to give you a title for the passage.

Key to Test 8

Reading Passage 1

Questions 1 – 6

1. **Answer: No**. The answer is in paragraph 1. The answer is at the end of the second sentence: ... *,and most recently, and its first excursion this century outside the literature of the Museum, in Christopher Hibbert's new biography of George III.*

2. **Answer: Yes**. The answer is in the last sentence of paragraph 2. The writer points out the review was anonymous when published and then gives the name of the person who wrote it.

3. **Answer: Yes**. The answer is in the last sentence of paragraph 2. See number 2.

4. **Answer: Yes**. The answer is in paragraph 3.

5. **Answer: No**. The answer is in paragraph 2. Note that Murray is the **publisher**. The book was written by Richard Ford.

6. **Answer: Not Given**. The text does not give any indication about the amount of money involved.

Questions 7 – 10

7. **Answer: King's library**. The answer is in paragraph 4. Note the answer is not *Notes & Queries.*

8. **Answer: munificent gift**. The answer is in paragraph 4.

9. **Answer: absolutely unfounded**. The answer is in paragraph 6.

10. **Answer: involved in the plan**. The answer is in paragraph 7.

Questions 11 – 14

11. **Answer: C**. The answer is at the beginning of paragraph 8.

12. **Answer: C**. The answer is in paragraph 8 in the part of the text that is inside the parenthesis at the end: *a suggestion ... that is ... supported by ....*

13. **Answer: B**. The answer is in the first sentence of the last paragraph. Note the word *obscure* means *unclear*.

14. **Answer: A**. The answer is in second sentence of the last paragraph. Note that the word *veteran* does not mean *old* here, but that Coker had been a politician for a long time.

Reading Passage 2

Questions 15 – 21

15. **Answer: vii.**

16. **Answer: vi.**

17. **Answer: xi.** Heading iv is not suitable as it does not really talk about the countryside, but the noise there. Nor is there any mention of beauty.

18. **Answer: viii.** Heading ix is not suitable as the paragraph does not just talk about restaurants.

19. **Answer: x.**

20. **Answer: iii.**

21. **Answer: i.**

Questions 22 – 27

Note that you can use **A** as the answer more than once.

22. **Answer: K.** The answer is at the end of paragraph B.

23. **Answer: A.** The passage does not give any solution for cinemas. See paragraph E.

24. **Answer: D.** The answer is in paragraph G. Restaurants are talked about in paragraph E, but the solution is given in paragraph G.

25. **Answer: F.** The answer is in paragraph G in the second sentence.

26. **Answer: L.** The answer is in paragraph D.

27. **Answer: A.** The passage does not give any solution for shops.

Reading Passage 3

Questions 28–31

The answers to this section are all in the first paragraph.

28. **Answer: No.**

29. **Answer: No.** Note that the text says *may deplore.* This sentence is in effect like the first sentence of an although clause: *Although they deplore, ...* . Note the word *But* at the beginning of the last sentence of the paragraph.

30. **Answer: No.** The answer is in the last two sentences of the paragraph.

31. **Answer: Not Given.**

Questions 32–40

32. **Answer: boon**. The answer is in paragraph 2.

33. **Answer: marginalised**. The answer is in paragraph 3. The word *peripheral* (in the fifth sentence in the third paragraph) cannot be used here, because the classics are not attacked for being so.

34. **Answer: elitist**. The answer is in paragraph 3, in the last sentence.

35. **Answer: damned**. The answer is in the first sentence of paragraph 4. Note that the word *tainted* does not fit here.

36. **Answer: irrelevant**. The answer is in the first sentence of paragraph 4.

37. **Answer: professional**. The answer is in paragraph 4.

38. **Answer: argument**. The answer is in the last sentence of paragraph 4.

39. **Answer: relevant/pertinent**. The first answer is in the last sentence of paragraph 4. The word *pertinent* is in paragraph 5.

40. **Answer: lost**. The answer is in paragraph 7.

Key to Test 9

Reading Passage 1

Questions 1 – 6

1. **Answer: xii**. The word *panacea* occurs in the paragraph, but the whole paragraph is not about this and so heading i is not the answer.

2. **Answer: iv**. Heading x is obviously wrong as it relates only to a detail in the last sentence of the paragraph.

3. **Answer: xiii**. The answer is not heading ii as this relates only to a part of the information in the paragraph, i.e. the second sentence.

4. **Answer: vii**. Note that heading vi is not the answer as the paragraph does not contrast needles with fingers. In the last sentence of the paragraph, it states only that shiatsu uses the same points and energy lines as acupuncture.

5. **Answer: xi**. The answer is not heading x, because it relates to only part of the information in the paragraph. It is information, which is subsidiary to the meaning of the whole paragraph. See the answer for paragraph C in 2 above.

6. **Answer: ix**. The answer is not heading v. Nor is heading vi the answer as the paragraph does not contrast the use of fingers and needles.

The passage is long, but the headings are fairly straightforward. Note also that there are fewer questions for this reading passage.

Questions 7 – 10

7. **Answer: D**. The answer is in paragraph C.

8. **Answer: H**. The answer is in paragraph D.

9. **Answer: B**. The answer is in paragraph E. Note that E is not the answer. Compare the information with the passage.

10. **Answer: C**. The answer is in paragraph G.

Reading Passage 2

Questions 11 – 18

Please note that the instructions allow you to use any heading more than once!

11. **Answer: iv**. Paragraph B talks about the problems relating to SATs. There is a hint in the first paragraph of the writer's antipathy to testing. Then, in paragraph B, he says that *SATs purport to* (i.e. claim to, with the claim being false!). Note how paragraph B is divided: look at the information before and after the word *But* in the middle of the paragraph. As the focus is on the latter part of the paragraph and given the use of the word *purport* as above, heading xi cannot be the answer.

12. **Answer: iv**. Paragraph C also talks about the problems relating to SATs! Be careful as the paragraph is not primarily about MCQs! The information relating to MCQs is subsidiary to the meaning of the whole paragraph, i.e. that there are problems with SATs.

13. **Answer: xii**. Paragraph D covers the failings of MCQs. It is very similar to Paragraphs B and C in this respect. It does not give the theory behind MCQs, so heading ii is not possible.

14. **Answer: xiv**. The distracter here is heading x. Note that the first sentence is only the introduction to the paragraph. Beware of just looking at first and last sentences to work out headings!

15. **Answer: i**. The distracter here is heading vi. The paragraph does not mention anything about a need for computer assessment.

16. **Answer: ix**. This should pose no problems.

17. **Answer: vii**. Heading v is not suitable, because it talks about psychometric testing in the future, not about misuse of testing in schools.

18. **Answer: viii**.

Questions 19 – 23

19. **Answer: an obsession/rather an obsession**. The answer is in the first paragraph. The word *obsession* indicates the writer's negative attitude towards testing which is indicated throughout the passage. See number 11 above.

20. **Answer: the United States**. The answer is in the first sentence of paragraph B.

21. **Answer: the better-off/better-off children/middle-class children**. The first answer is in the first sentence of paragraph. C. The second answer is in the second sentence of paragraph. C. Note the answer is not *poor students,* which is found at the beginning of the second paragraph. The tests only claim to help such students; the writer does not say that they do so. Note the word limit.

22. **Answer: [the] convenience**. The answer is in the last sentence of paragraph F.

23. **Answer: the workplace**. The answer is in the first sentence of paragraph G.

Questions 24 – 26

24. **Answer: No**. The answer is in the last sentence of paragraph G.

25. **Answer: Not Given**. The text does not say anything about the information in this statement.

26. **Answer: Yes**. There is evidence throughout the passage. For example, look at 11 and 19 above.

Reading Passage 3

Questions 27–32

27. **Answer: Not Given**. The first sentence of the first paragraph tells us that *Wittgenstein has been regarded as one of the major philosophers .....* The text does not tell us whether Wittgenstein was a moral philosopher or not.

28. **Answer: Yes**. The answer is in paragraph 1.

29. **Answer: No**. The answer is in paragraph 2: *Wittgenstein is both highly critical and at the same time greatly admiring ...* . Therefore, his admiration is not total.

30. **Answer: No**. See the end of paragraph 2.

31. **Answer: Not Given**. The text does not say anywhere whether other people support Freud's theory or not.

32. **Answer: Yes**. The answer is at the end of the third paragraph. Note *behoves us* means *we must*.

Questions 33–40

Remember to read through the summary to check the type of word that is required. All of the words come from the last paragraph.

33. **Answer: Freud's**. Note the word *his* at the end of the sentence, which should indicate that a name is required here.

34. **Answer: explaining**

35. **Answer: redescribing**.

36. **Answer: picture**.

37. **Answer: therapeutic**.

38. **Answer: unique**

39. **Answer: patient**

40. **Answer: insight(s)**.

Key to Test 10

Reading Passage 1

Questions 1–4

1. **Answer: redeeming features.** The answer is in the first sentence of the second paragraph. Note that the word **no** is not needed in the answer.

2. **Answer: overreact/ they overreact/tend to overreact**. The answer is in the fourth sentence of the second paragraph.

3. **Answer: a bad name**. The answer is in the first sentence of the third paragraph.

4. **Answer: redress the balance**. The answer is in the fourth paragraph.

Questions 5 – 10

The answers for this section are found in the fifth and sixth paragraphs.

5. **Answer: order/insect order**.

6. **Answer: problem(s)**.

7. **Answer: pest control/control**. Note you cannot put the word *natural* here as you would then exceed the word limit. The phrase *natural control programmes* would not work either. The second answer is possible, but not is not as good as the first one.

8. **Answer: queen/single queen**.

9. **Answer: aggressive**.

10. **Answer: defensive**.

Questions 11 – 16

The answers for this section are found in the seventh paragraph.

11. **Answer: emerge**.

12. **Answer: grubs/eggs**.

13 **Answer: larvae**.

14. **Answer: mate**.

15. **Answer: perishes/dies.**

16. **Answer: hibernation**.

Reading Passage 2

Questions 17 – 24

The headings in this section should not be too difficult. However, there are more of them to choose from, which may make the exercise appear difficult.

17. **Answer: i**. Heading xi is obviously wrong, because it relates only to part of the paragraph and is subsidiary to the main idea. Nor is xiii correct for the same reason.

18. **Answer: vi**.

19. **Answer: ix**. Heading ii is obviously wrong, as it is the other way round. Nor is xvi suitable, as it is an afterthought added on to the second example of the paragraph. Does it relate to the surgery example?

20. **Answer: x**. Heading xv relates only to a detail in the paragraph, so it is obviously wrong.

21. **Answer: iv**.

22. **Answer: xiv**.

23. **Answer: iii**. Heading v is wrong, as it is just a phrase lifted from the paragraph.

24. **Answer: xii**. Heading viii is obviously wrong, as it relates only to a detail. Keep this heading in your head and read through the paragraph. Does it summarise all the information?

Questions 25 – 27

25. **Answer: Yes**. The answer is in the first sentence of paragraph C.

26. **Answer: Not Given**. Look at paragraph E. There is no mention of the information in this statement.

27. **Answer: No**. This is obvious from the whole passage. See especially the last paragraph.

Reading Passage 3

Questions 28–33

28. **Answer: No**. The answer may be found in the second sentence of the first paragraph.

29. **Answer: Yes**. The answer may be found at the end of the first paragraph.

30. **Answer: Yes**. The answer may be found at the end of the first paragraph and the first sentence of the second paragraph.

31. **Answer: Yes**. The answer may be found in the second paragraph. The paragraph gives you a brief tour of the Gallery.

32. **Answer: Not Given**. There is no indication in the passage about the reaction of spectators.

33. **Answer: No**. The answer may be found in the middle of the second paragraph. Note the word *mock* means *make fun of*.

Questions 34–37

34. **Answer: C**. The answer may be found in the second paragraph. You need to check the whole paragraph. **A** and **B** are obviously wrong, as the Gallery contains a range of different types of paintings (compare this question with number 31 above), which come from different periods. As for **D**, there is no mention of this in the text.
35. **Answer: A**. The answer may be found in the second paragraph. Compare this question with 30. The answer to this question gives a specific example of the general idea of the article as expressed in number 30. **B** is not correct, because the passage does not say this as regards the Gallery – remember that the removal of the icons to the Gallery was done to minimise the religious aspect of the icons. **C** is not correct, because it is the direct opposite. Alternative **D** is not mentioned in the passage.
36. **Answer: A**. The answer may be found at the end of the second sentence in the third paragraph. The text says *icons mainly from the 15th to the 17th century*, so **B** cannot be true. As for **C**, the passage does not say anything about this. If you look at the last sentence of the third paragraph you can see that the monastery building was not destroyed, so **D** is wrong.
37. **Answer: C**. The answer may be found in the last sentence of the third paragraph. Note that **A** is not the correct answer, as the original architects are not praised. Alternatives **B** and **D** are obviously wrong.

Questions 38–40

38. **Answer: human motherhood**. The answer is in the second sentence of the penultimate paragraph. Note the answer is not *Mother of God*.
39. **Answer: humanistic interpretation**. The answer is found in the fourth sentence of the last paragraph.
40. **Answer: hero**. The answer is in the last sentence of the last paragraph.

Appendix

IELTS Reading Answer Sheet

Module taken (shade one box below):

Academic ▭ General Training ▭

Version number: Please enter the number in the boxes and shade the number in the grid.

0 1 2 3 4 5 6 7 8 9

0 1 2 3 4 5 6 7 8 9

		√	X
1		▭ 1	▭
2		▭ 2	▭
3		▭ 3	▭
4		▭ 4	▭
5		▭ 5	▭
6		▭ 6	▭
7		▭ 7	▭
8		▭ 8	▭
9		▭ 9	▭
10		▭ 10	▭
11		▭ 11	▭
12		▭ 12	▭
13		▭ 13	▭
14		▭ 14	▭
15		▭ 15	▭
16		▭ 16	▭
17		▭ 17	▭
18		▭ 18	▭
19		▭ 19	▭
20		▭ 20	▭
21		▭ 21	▭
22		▭ 22	▭
23		▭ 23	▭
24		▭ 24	▭
25		▭ 25	▭
26		▭ 26	▭
27		▭ 27	▭
28		▭ 28	▭
29		▭ 29	▭
30		▭ 30	▭

		√	X
31		▭ 31	▭
32		▭ 32	▭
33		▭ 33	▭
34		▭ 34	▭
35		▭ 35	▭
36		▭ 36	▭
37		▭ 37	▭
38		▭ 38	▭
39		▭ 39	▭
40		▭ 40	▭

Band Score		Listening Total	

Marker's Initials	

Reproduced by permission of the University of Cambridge Local Examinations Syndicate